ISBN 978-0-266-19086-8
PIBN 10188298

State Library Building.

DEDICATION

OF THE

STATE LIBRARY BUILDING

AT

CONCORD, NEW HAMPSHIRE

TUESDAY, JANUARY 8, 1895

Published by Authority of the State

CONCORD

EDWARD N. PEARSON, PUBLIC PRINTER

1895

LAWS OF 1895, CHAPTER 125.

JOINT RESOLUTION PROVIDING FOR THE PRINTING OF THE PRO-
CEEDINGS AT THE DEDICATION OF THE STATE LIBRARY BUILD-
ING, JANUARY 8, 1895.

Resolved by the Senate and House of Representatives in General Court convened:

That the governor and council be requested to procure the printing of two thousand copies of the proceedings at the dedication of the state library building at Concord, January 8, 1895, including the addresses of William J. Tucker and Ainsworth R. Spofford, with suitable cuts of the exterior and interior of the building.

CONTENTS.

CONTENTS.

INTRODUCTION.

New Hampshire, in assuming to do for the people what the people formerly accomplished for themselves, has made progress only after demonstration that paternalism in government does not trespass upon the theory and practice of a pure democracy. The progress of thought and the enlargement of practice have founded state institutions and generally have granted privileges and facilities which individually the people could not secure for themselves. The internal history of the state library reveals an origin and development in harmony with a liberal interpretation of the functions of a wise and comprehensive state administration.

So long as the library remained under the immediate control and supervision of the legislature its growth was dwarfed and its functions were limited to a narrow sphere. In 1866, under more liberal legislation, the library became an institution with a permanent board of control, and during the succeeding years it has profited under the fostering care of the state. Within thirty years the number of volumes has been increased tenfold, and the interest of the public has kept an even pace with the rapid progress of the library.

In the early history of the state, there was no state library or thought of one. Until 1816 there was no state house nor any public building in which a state library could be sheltered. During the first twenty years under the constitution, the legislature held only

two successive sessions in the same town, and these
were special and not annual sessions. During the
years preceding the establishment of a permanent seat
of government, it is evident the state was not saving and
moving books from town to town. The treasurer was
summoned to attend with the iron chest wherever the
general court pitched its tent, but no library was trans-
ported from one temporary capital to another. The
state had none. If we claim for the institution the
added glory of antiquity, we must admit that in its
imaginative existence it was vehicular. With the completion and occupancy of a permanent state house, it is
probable that a few books were collected, but it was
several years before the state entertained any thought of
a permanent library, or even reserved a copy of its own
publications for its use. The Journals of the Senate and
House of Representatives, and other volumes, published
by the state, previous to 1826, and now in the state
library, were secured by donation or purchase at a later
date.

For the first time the state library receives mention in
the state records in an act of 1823 appropriating $100
annually for its enlargement. The poverty of the institution is revealed in an act of 1826 which provided for
the purchase of " one copy of the Journal of the Senate
and House of Representatives for each session since the
adoption of the present constitution."

In 1828 Jacob Bailey Moore was appointed an agent
to prepare a room under the senate chamber for the
accommodation of the state library. Mr. Moore caused
to be arranged a series of shelves in a long, narrow
room across the north end of the state house, and here
the library remained until the autumn of 1864. An act
of 1848 provided for the removal of the library to the
west side of the state house, but no action was taken on

account of a failure of the general court to make an adequate appropriation for the purpose.

In 1828 the whole number of volumes was less than 600. These were packed rather than shelved in limited accommodations, and the door was securely locked the greater part of the year. During the succeeding fifteen years about an equal number of volumes of a miscellaneous character was added to the originals, and with them committed to a continued and solitary confinement.

The only printed catalogue of the state library was issued nearly fifty years ago. An act approved June 30, 1846, directed the secretary of state, the librarian, *ex-officio*, to print three hundred copies of a catalogue of the library. The catalogue demonstrates that the collection of statutes and legislative journals of the United States and of the several states, had been considerably increased within the few years immediately preceding. At this date the library also contained nearly 400 law reports, digests, and works of an elementary character. In the miscellaneous department there were about 600 volumes of history, biography, and reference books.

At the June session, 1849, Alexandre Vattemare, of Paris, delivered an address before the legislature, advocating an international exchange of public documents. The address was printed at the expense of the state, and a joint resolution was passed directing the librarian to present Mr. Vattemare "such copies of the Journals of the legislature and other volumes and pamphlets in his possession as in his opinion can be consistently thus appropriated." In exchange the library received in uniform and substantial bindings 125 volumes in French. They are silent reminders of a policy suddenly adopted, and as speedily relinquished.

In 1834, Jacob C. Carter was chosen librarian, and by annual elections was continued in office until the close of the session of 1846. During this period, and for many succeeding years, the library was opened only during the session and for the sole accommodation of the legislature and the state officers. An act of 1846 changed the form, but not the spirit, of the control of the library. The secretary of state became the librarian *ex-officio* with authority to appoint a special deputy to open the library during the session, and in 1857 the deputy secretary of state was made librarian *ex-officio*, and continued to discharge the limited duties of the office until 1866.

The state house was re-modelled between the special session in August, 1864, and the June session, 1866. In the meantime the books of the state library were stored in the basement of the city hall. They were removed from the state house in the autumn of 1864, eighty years after the adoption of the state constitution. At this time it could be called a library only by courtesy. At best it was a broken collection of law books and state documents with a very few volumes of a miscellaneous character. The repairs upon the state house provided a room for the library upon the centre of the west side. It was left unfinished, and the books remained in storage until the summer of 1867. During eighty years the legislature practically retained the immediate control and supervision of the library. The laws were temporary in their character and to no one was delegated an authority to secure any permanent results. Each annual session legislated for its immediate convenience, often doing too much for a month and always too little for a year.

At the June session, 1866, the legislature assembled in the re-modeled state house. It was the beginning of an era in the history of the library. The spirit of the prophet was breathing in the dead bones in the valley, and the voice of progress called the people to the opened doors of the library. Under the provisions of the act of 1866 the state library was enlarged from a legislative convenience to a public institution. The control was delegated to a perpetual board of trustees, and a more liberal provision was made for its support. Under this management the room provided was completed and a permanent librarian was appointed. The results were immediate and constant, and the library soon outgrew the accommodations provided by the trustees. The situation found frequent expression in the legislature without results until the session of 1889, in the passage of a joint resolution authorizing the governor and council to procure plans and estimates for the enlargement of the state house or the erection of a separate building for the accommodation of the library. Under this authority the governor and council appointed Charles H. Burns, John W. Sanborn, Benjamin A. Kimball, Irving W. Drew, and Charles J. Amidon. The commission held frequent sessions, and industriously prosecuted the work of inquiry and investigation. To the succeeding legislature they recommended a site, and presented plans and estimates for a new building. The plan contained provision for a court room and adjoining rooms for the accommodation of the court and members of the bar. The recommendations of the commission were promptly accepted by the legislature, and without opposition an act was passed authorizing the governor and council to appoint four commissioners to erect a building in accordance with the accepted plans and upon the proposed site. The commission under the act of 1889 consisted of five members, and with the knowledge of the desire of Mr. Amidon to be excused from further service, the building commission under the act of 1891 comprised four members. The governor and council appointed Charles H. Burns, John W. Sanborn,

Benjamin A. Kimball, and Irving W. Drew commissioners for the erection of the new building. The plans
accepted were those of A. P. Cutting of Worcester,
Mass., and he remained associated with the commissioners during the construction of the building. The
liberality of the people as expressed in legislation, and
the wisdom of the commissioners are fittingly expressed
in the fair proportions and the spacious accommodation
of an attractive and durable structure.

The state library enters upon a new era of its existence with hope and confidence. During the past
twenty-eight years, under the management of the
trustees, its growth has been uniform and constant.
It now contains, exclusive of duplicates, 50,000 volumes,
of which 14,000 are in the law department. Including
pamphlets, state and United States documents, it pos-
sesses over 100,000 duplicates. Every year is adding
more volumes than the library contained fifty years ago.

The Main Hall.

THE STATE LIBRARY BUILDING.

The problem as received from the commissioners was for a building, first, to contain and accommodate the state library, with ample means for immediate growth within its walls, and so arranged that a stack room for future growth could be added, retaining the present structure for administrative purposes, with reading room of ample dimensions for its prospective growth for many years to come.

Second, to provide rooms for the supreme court of the state, comprising court room, judges' consultation and private rooms, clerks' and attorneys' room, with such additional rooms as would naturally grow out of the development of the scheme, and suitable for offices under the state government, and the whole to be of the most substantial character, as nearly fireproof as consistent with available use.

It is not necessary to minutely describe all the intricate details entering into the construction of the building, but in any description, however brief, it should not be overlooked that the foundations are laid deep and strong; that the materials were carefully selected and of the best quality available; that each and every one of the intricate details have in turn received all, and much more care and thought than is usually expended upon such problems; that the building not only looks strong and permanent, but it has really greater strength than is apparent, for by the solid character of the backing of the exterior walls and by the tying into them of the solid masonry partitions, which buttress them in every direction and add untold strength to its otherwise massive solidity ; that in heating, lighting, ventilation, and sanitation it is the best that expert service can give ; in decoration and ornament it is true to the style selected. That it is not highly decorated, is true, for both its material and purpose forbid such a course.

It is situated fronting the state-house grounds from the north , with a frontage on Park street of 141 feet 6 inches, on State street, 104 feet 2 inches, with a width of 94 feet 4 inches at the narrowest point through the library east of the main entrance, with a slight projecting tower 24 feet square at the southwest corner, one story higher than the main building, with a high, pitched roof; a segmental bay from the centre of the court room at the west end, and a semi-circular bay at the right of the main entrance with finish membering into and joining the same. The extreme height of main walls from grade is 44 feet, with a gable over main entrance 57 feet in height, and a tower 83 feet in height.

The exterior is wholly of New Hampshire granite in two colors. The body of the work and basement entire are of Conway red granite, rock face, except reveals and mouldings which are fine cut. The trimmings comprising all belts, mouldings, pilasters, cornices, copings, entrance steps, etc., are of Concord gray granite, and wholly dressed work. The backing of all exterior walls and partitions is of brick laid in cement.

The framing of floors, ceilings, roof trusses, stairs, columns, entire, are of steel. The floors, columns, ceilings, and roof are filled with burnt clay tiles, with projecting flanges wholly enclosing metal construction, by a solid covering of previously burnt materials. The floors and roof arches are filled and leveled with concrete to receive floors and roof covering.

The floors for vestibule, main hall first and second stories, and border of court room are of marble mosaic, and all other floors marble tiles.

The roof has a waterproof covering over masonry construction overlaid with seven-eighths inch planed slates bedded in mastic. Flashing and skylight ribs are of copper. Skylights are glazed with one-half inch thick, hammered plate glass, with all windows glazed with thick, polished plate glass.

The plastering is laid directly to masonry construction. The door and window trimmings for the vestibule, main and staircase halls, and court room are of polished marble; all other trimmings are of Keene cement. The book cases and stacks are of iron. Wood is only used for door and window casements and furniture is mainly quartered oak, and is of so inconsiderable an amount that the whole could be burned in any room in the building without endangering its construction.

The basement has a strong battered wall 6 feet 9 inches in height, of unusually large stone, springing from a solid underpinning with projecting wash and terminating with a belt 3 feet wide of three members, base, die, and sill course, running entirely around the building.

From this belt of light colored granite spring pilasters 2 feet 6 inches wide projecting 6 inches, with moulded base and delicately carved capitals, coupled at the angles, single at each division or bay, around the building and running up to and supporting the main cornice. The motive of the main cornice is Grecian, 4 feet in width, composed of frieze, dentils, egg and dart, bed moulding, facia and corona. Over the main cornice is a sort of battlement wall 3 feet 3 inches in height, of red granite trimmed with gray, forming roof stop.

The segmental bay at the west end back of the judges' bench from the court room, is pierced with triple windows standing high up on massive panels of red granite, with rugged split faces. The spandrils over the same windows have similar panels surrounded by ornamental mouldings. Through the curtain walls between the pilasters are the windows for the first and second stories, with moulded panels between them, giving the effect of connected windows. The lower ones have stone mullions and transoms, and the second semi-circular tops.

The rear entrance to the library from the north and the hatchway to the basement, while absolutely without ornament, are wonderfully interesting, showing as they do the massive strength of the work.

The main entrance is from Park street in the south front, 53 feet from the southwest corner to the centre. The entrance is composed of thirteen granite steps 20 feet wide, solidly buttressed at either side and flanked with massive stone piers 6 feet 3 inches wide up to the height of first story, from which spring coupled pilasters running up to and supporting gable cornice above the battlements walls of the main building. The tympanum, formed by the pitch of the gable, is richly carved, the central motive of which is the modified state seal.

Standing between the main piers of the first story and the pilasters of the second, are four pairs of coupled columns, one standing back of the other. These columns are polished and of green granite from Conway quarries. The lower ones have pedestals membering with the belt extending around the building, with moulded bases and delicately carved capitals, and support the massive stone lintel 2 feet high, 3 feet 9 inches wide, and 18 feet long, over which rests the die bearing the inscription in polished letters " STATE LIBRARY." The die and its capping form guard. for upper balcony, and from which spring

companion columns supporting the great arch over the
balcony. The portico and balcony over it are faced
with granite with floors and ceilings of solid granite
flags.

The motive of the exterior, as it finds expression in its
coursed ashlar walls, mouldings, panels, cornices, pilasters, etc., is of the early Italian renaissance period,
which originated near the end of the fifteenth century, at
a time when the great masters of Italian art had grown
weary of the Byzantine, Gothic, and Romanesque, and
were reaching out into new fields and gaining fresh con-
quests in their chosen profession, receiving their inspiration from Grecian art of 2,000 years before; their works
were so successful that they have ever since found expression in the best works of every European country,
and are steadily gaining in favor at home. While in the
whole there is scarcely a new thing in the builders' art,
the adaptation to its purpose is quite unusual in architecture, and the whole gives the impression of great
solidity as if built for eternity.

From the main porch through double doors of polished
oak surrounded by transoms and side lights, we pass
through a vestibule 5 feet 6 inches by 22 feet, and enter
the main hall by similar doors. This hall is 22 feet by 74
feet 6 inches, running through and receiving its light
from the triple windows over the main staircase in the
rear wall, and forms a dividing line between the two
departments of the building, at the right of which is the
library and at the left the court departments.

From this hall by two pairs of double doors at the
right, we enter the great reading room of the library.
This room is 42 feet wide, 70 feet 8 inches long, and 34
feet 6 inches high; is flanked on either side by a colonnade of six Grecian Doric columns surmounted by a
classic entablature, which supports a similar colonnade

with Grecian columns with composite capitals, with intersecting arches, beams in the first story and arches in the second story, intersecting with pilasters on the outer walls of the room, extending up to the main ceiling.

The columns forming the second story colonnade are connected between them, as well as at the ends, with marble rails, supported on ornamental wrought iron balustrade. These columns are 9 feet from the alcove walls, and are designed to form separating corridors between the alcoves and the central section of the main reading room, which is lighted with large windows at the east end and skylight comprising nearly the whole central section of the ceiling. The second story colonnade with the attendant balustrade forms galleries around the room from which the second story alcoves are reached.

In entering the library at the first door, at the right is an attendant staircase from the basement to the second story. Adjoining this is a trustees' room, the extreme dimensions of which are 16 feet by 30 feet, with the outer end occupying the semi-circular bay, which is pierced with a group of five transomed windows. Of the remaining four alcoves upon the right hand or south side, three are 10 feet 2 inches by 22 feet and the fourth is 13 feet by 22 feet. The three central alcoves on the north side are of the same dimensions as the south side, while opposite the trustees' room is a vault 13 feet 6 inches by 16 feet 8 inches, constructed of hard brick with 3-foot walls laid solid in cement. At the northwest corner of the library department, and connected with a driveway from the rear entrance, is a staircase connecting with basement, and with first and second stories.

The alcoves in the library department are each 14 feet in the clear height, giving the requisite height for two tiers of bookcases, when the same shall be required, and are each lighted from end walls by large windows surrounded

The Court Room.

by bookcases and provided with reading tables and chairs, forming a series of reading rooms for classified books.

The basement immediately under the library department has faced and jointed lining walls and. piers of brick, with a metalithic concrete floor covering the whole space. The whole is amply lighted and used for book storage and supplies. Between the basement staircase and the main library the two alcoves on the right are fitted for cataloguing purposes.

At the left of the main hall by the first door we reach the judges' consultation room, 19 feet by 22 feet 3 inches, through which we reach a private office, 15 feet 8 inches square, in the space occupied by the tower. From either of these rooms through a lobby 7 feet by 9 feet 5 inches, entrance to the court room is formed. Outside of this lobby is the judges' lavatory, of similar size. Through the next three doors from the hall, a wide one in the centre, flanked on either side by single doors, we enter the court room, 36 feet by 50 feet by 26 feet 6 inches high, with a segmental bay in the immediate front. The windows of the bay stand high up over the judges' bench, which is located 9 feet from the outer wall.

Connecting with the court room from the northwest corner of the building is a clerk's room, about 17 feet square, with vault. Adjoining this room and connecting with main hall is a similar room for consultation.

At the rear end of the main hall at the right, is the main staircase, 9 feet wide, constructed of iron and marble, and leading to the second story, and connecting directly with the second story reception hall, 22 feet by 57 feet 9 inches, which is surrounded by a finely ornamented cornice, with semi-circular glazed ceiling with extreme height of 26 feet. From this hall, through a glazed par-

tition, the balcony over the main porch is reached. The
light of this room is admirably adapted for the exhibi-
tion of paintings, views, and other objects of art.
Through this room are reached the gallery in the library
and the second story rooms occupying the space used by
the judges in the lower floor, comprising rooms 19 feet by
22 feet 3 inches, 15 feet 8 inches square, and 9 feet 5
inches by 15 feet, and from the landing in the main staircase at the north side of the building a room 17 feet by 36
feet, thus completing the appointments of the building.

The heating and ventilating of the building are accomplished by a power system, consisting of two horizontal
locomotive boilers with heating coils, and a fan driven
by electric power. These are located under the main
hall, and are absolutely disconnected from the library
department, except the heating conduits. The cold air
is taken from high up in the north wall, and conducted
by the solid masonry conduits to the heating coils
through the fan to the distributing conduits. The system includes mixing dampers with thermostats and electric control, and as computed by the manufacturers is
rated at 25,000 cubic feet of fresh air per minute. By
the electric control a change of two degrees in temper-
ature only is required to open or close the hot and cold
air supply.

The computation of ventilating flues provides for a
capacity sufficient to change the air in the court room
every ten minutes, and in the library every fifteen
minutes.

The vestibule, main and staircase halls have a rich
wainscot 5 feet 6 inches high of Sienna marble with base
and cap mouldings, door and window trimmings of
Verona red marble, extending up the main staircase to
the second story, and including the triple windows over
the staircase.

Midway between the doors to the library is a massive mantel of Grecian design, and like the hall surrounding it, is of Sienna marble, with Verona red trimmings, the motive of which is solid paneled pilasters relieved with decorated mouldings up to and supporting the shelf, above which spring coupled fluted pilasters with rich capitals carrying the main entablature.

The space over the shelf between pilasters to the cornice, is filled with a bronze panel bearing the names of those officials who have been instrumental in the building's erection, surrounded by symbolic carvings in bas-relief.

The floors of main hall and vestibule are mosaic, of colored marble, with rich borders and centre pieces.

The space at the rear end of the main hall under the staircase is occupied for a general lavatory.

In the reading room of the library, opposite the mantel in the hall, is the companion fireplace of white marble, of classic design, the motive of which is two pairs of entasised composite columns, with delicately carved capitals 8 feet in diameter, and 7 feet 10 inches high, supporting classic entablature with decorated mouldings, with mantel shelf terminating between them. Over the centre and supported by main entablature is a marble clock, designed in harmony with the mantel.

The main reading room in the library has Italian marble wainscot 3 feet 6 inches high, intersecting with the pedestals of wall pilasters, and matching the independent pedestals of the main colonnade. All the finish above the wainscot is of Keene cement, and the floors of the reading room and alcoves connected with the same are of marble tiles.

The court-room floor is surrounded by a colored marble mosaic border, moderately decorated, with the central floor covered with concrete and overlaid with rich carpet. The room has marble wainscot 5 feet 1 1-2 inches in height, intersecting with the two marble mantels at either end, and with door and window trimmings, the whole of carefully selected Italian vein marble.

The mantels have coupled Grecian Doric columns, decorated with egg and dart mouldings, at either side, supporting shelves.

Through the main wall back of the columns are grilled registers connected with main flues for ventilation.

The fireplaces are also designed for heating the building in moderate weather, and supplement the main flues for ventilation.

The room has an intermediate cornice 13 feet from the floor, forming capping over doors and windows and encircling the room, from which spring fluted pilasters with composite Grecian capitals, supporting the main cornice, which is also decorated with Grecian ornamental mouldings. From the centre of the court room ceiling springs an elliptical dome 28 feet in diameter, with ribbed and paneled soffit springing up to and receiving light from the ceiling through an ornamental circular ceiling light 13 feet in diameter. The judges' bench, standing on marble base 15 feet in height, is of classic design in solid mahogany.

The furniture throughout is of oak in general harmony with the work, and of excellent quality.

The main rooms in the building are provided with fireplaces with marble mantels of simple design, which will be found of advantage in heating the rooms in moderate weather, and in aiding materially in the general ventilation of the building.

The system of artificial lighting is for a combination of both gas and electricity, and the fixtures were designed for the building. The wiring for electric lights is a full line of metal-armored conduits starting from the basement, and from which every wire in the building . can be introduced or removed. The fixtures comprise a row of lights every thirty inches around the cornice of the lower colonnade in the library, with brackets from the walls in the first and second stories. Each alcove is lighted with independent chandeliers. The second story hall is lighted in a manner similar to the library, by a row of lights supported by and suspended from the main cornice at spring of circular ceiling, rendering the room suitable for the display of works of art.

The court room has a series of electric lights around the upper and lower members of the dome, and brackets at the right and left of the judges' bench.

The main hall has brackets on the court room side, with candelabra of elaborate design at either side of the mantel.

Springing from the walls at either side of the portico and back of the piers and columns, are a pair of solid bronze brackets carrying electric lights, the models for which originated in Southern Italy, and their prototypes used for another purpose will be found in the Metropolitan Museum of Fine Arts, in New York city. They find so fitting place through the personal efforts of a member of the commission. The reflected electric light from them shows with effect the tri-colored granite, of which the portico is composed.

When the interior of the building shall have received the simple color decoration of soft gray, illuminated with slight touches of higher color and gold to properly emphasize its details; when time shall have softened its exterior tones, and overgrown its lawns with a few choice vines and shrubs, giving to its exterior the charm of age; when the same softening influences shall have removed from the interior the slight resonance always incident to new work; when the walls and every available space shall be filled with cases, and the cases filled to overflowing with the choicest works of law, literature, and art; when the daily throng of those seeking knowledge where knowledge can be best obtained shall be welcomed; then, and not till then, will the full measure of its usefulness, and the wisdom of its promoters and of the commonwealth that so generously provided for it, be fully realized.

TRUSTEES.

Under the provisions of the Act of 1866, the trustees (except two of the first appointments) are appointed for the term of three years, and one is appointed each year. The following is a record of appointments :

1866. Asa McFarland, declined to serve.
1866. George Stark, for three years.
1866. Nicholas V. Whitehouse, for two years.
1866. Parsons B. Cogswell, for one year.
1867. Parsons B. Cogswell, for three years.
1868. William L. Foster, for three years.
1869. George Stark, for three years.
1870. Parsons B. Cogswell, for three years.
1871. William L. Foster, for three years.
1872. George Stark, for three years.
1873. Parsons B. Cogswell, for three years.
1874. William M. Chase, for three years.
1875. George Stark, for three years.
1876. Parsons B. Cogswell, for three years.
1877. William M. Chase, for three years.
1878. George Stark, resigned 1879.
1879. William L. Foster, for two years.
1880. William M. Chase, for three years.
1881. William L. Foster, for three years.
1882. Austin F. Pike, for three years.
1883. William M. Chase, for three years.
1884. William L. Foster, for three years.
1885. Amos Hadley, for three years.

1886.   William M. Chase, resigned 1888.
1887.   Charles R. Corning, for three years.
1888.   Albert S. Batchellor, for one year.
1888.   George C. Gilmore, for three years.
1889.   Albert S. Batchellor, for three years.
1890.   Charles R. Corning, for three years.
1891.   George C. Gilmore, for three years.
1892.   Albert S. Batchellor, for three years.
1893.   Frank S. Streeter, for three years.
1894.   George C. Gilmore, for three years.
1895.   Albert S. Bachellor, for three years.

LIBRARIANS.

1834–1846. Jacob C. Carter, chosen by the legislature.
1846–1847. George G. Fogg, secretary of state, *ex-officio*.
1847–1850. Thomas P. Treadwell, secretary of state, *ex-officio*.
1850–1855. John L. Hadley, secretary of state, *ex-officio*.
1855–1857. Lemuel N. Pattee, secretary of state, *ex-officio*.
1857–1858. Nathan W. Gove, deputy secretary of state, *ex-officio*.
1858–1861. Allen Tenney, deputy secretary of state, *ex-officio*.
1861–1862. George H. Chandler, deputy secretary of state, *ex-officio*.
1862–1864. Benjamin Gerrish, deputy secretary of state, *ex-officio*.
1864–1865. James H. Burpee, deputy secretary of state, *ex-officio*.
1865–1866. Nathan W. Gove, deputy secretary of state, *ex-officio*.
1866–1867. Vacancy.
1867–1871. William H. Kimball, appointed by trustees.
1871–1872. Mitchell Gilmore, appointed by trustees.
1872–1890. William H. Kimball, appointed by trustees.
1890–1894. Arthur R. Kimball, appointed by trustees.
1894––––. Arthur H. Chase, appointed by trustees.

THE DEDICATION.

The State Library Building was formally dedicated Tuesday, January 8, 1895. The general arrangements were made by Governor Smith and his Council acting in concurrence with the commissioners, and will be fully set forth in the following narrative of the proceedings. The audience was large, filling the spacious building to its utmost limit, and included many distinguished guests from New Hampshire and from other states.

The exercises were formally opened at one o'clock by Harry G. Sargent, Esq., of Concord, the marshal of the day, who introduced as president Hon. J. S. H. Frink, of Greenland. Mr. Frink spoke as follows :

PRESIDENT'S ADDRESS.

No "loyal lover of letters" can approach and enter this magnificent edifice, which we to-day dedicate to literature and law, without a feeling of pride and gratification.

Without any analysis of the architectural design of the building, we feel, at once, that it is "comely" to look upon.

I know not whether the capitals, those upper members of the columns and pilasters that adorn its
outer and inner walls, are Ionic or Doric or Romanesque or English, but I do know, that this building
answers the prime purpose of true architecture; a
beautiful and harmonious adaptation to the purposes
for which it was designed.

There is a realism about it and its appointments,
an apparent absence of surrender of utility to orna-
mentation, such a blending of the beautiful and
the useful, as to make it very satisfactory to one who
studies its details.

Let me say, however, parenthetically, that obvi-
ously, one of the purposes for which this room was
designed, was not to accommodate this large audience.

Gratifying and acceptable, as is this library building,
yet it is not so much this result of the state's munificence, and the commissioners' taste,—this beautiful
achievement of stone and mortar,—that awakens our
thankfulness, as the implied assurance of an increasing and abiding interest of our people in the cause of
a higher education and, consequently, a better
government.

From this day the State's Library is assured of an
invigorated and healthier life. The commonwealth,
by the erection and dedication of this building, gives
a pledge of a more active assumption of its duties,
towards this, one of its most worthy beneficiaries.
To be sure, if our little library should enjoy the most
abundant prosperity that its warmest patron could
reasonably expect, it will always remain, *compara-*

tively an *inconsiderable* collection of books; yet it will serve well all the purposes of our community.

The legislator intent upon forecasting the future from the lessons of the past; the public official seeking some guidance in his duty, and the jurist striving to solve the enigmas of the law; and whoever may be interested in the religious, social, scientific, or political problems of the day, will find abundant counselors here, whose advice is wise, because born of experience.

> " That place that does contain
> My books—my best companions—is to me
> A glorious court, where hourly I converse
> With the old sages and philosophers,
> And sometimes for variety, I confer
> With kings and emperors, and weigh their counsels."

If this event should awaken an interest in historical investigation, the origin of this library will furnish a subject of interest to our local historians. It seems to be involved in some obscurity. Encyclopaedists and bibliographers credit it with a birth antedating our state government. Without investigation, and upon general principles, I assume that this belief is well founded. New Hampshire has never been credited, historically, with more than she deserved. In fact, we all know that a disposition has sometimes been manifested by some of her sister states to appropriate her renown.

With an editor of our State Papers, who has subdued the most fanciful imagination and grotesque humor of any story teller in the state, that he might become the most zealous and accurate of historians;

with a new librarian, who has abandoned a profession, in which he might have succeeded to the honors of his father, to become a companion of books; and with an assistant, who imbibed from his revered parent,—the former custodian of this library,—a personal acquaintance with every book and manuscript contained in it; certainly we ought not to want for some one who has the ability and interest to pursue this investigation.

New Hampshire, although far removed from the great intellectual and commercial centres of our country, has been a "quasi" pioneer in the encouragement of public libraries. Our legislative enactment of 1849, authorizing towns to appropriate money to establish and maintain libraries within their limits, was the first public statutory law in the states to this end. Our legislature has never been niggardly in its appropriations for public institutions of learning within the borders of the state. Its munificence has reached its climax in the erection of this much needed and greatly admired structure, which will stand for years as a monument of architectural propriety and state pride.

But we dedicate this building to-day to jurisprudence as well as to letters. Many of you have visited personally the court room. If you have not, I wish I could give you a pen picture of its many beauties and conveniences, but I am inadequate to the task.

I can only say in a general way, that in its symmetrical proportions, its elegant yet chaste adornments, and rich but substantial furnishings, it has no peer in New England, if in this country.

The character of this room and all its surround-
ings is so *honestly* adapted to the purposes for
which they are intended, that they would seem to
act as constant monitors to its professional occupants,
that "ways that are dark and tricks that are vain"
are inharmonious with the clear light and wholesome
atmosphere of such an apartment.

Of the site of this building, we can say with the
psalmist, it is "beautiful for situation." It occupies
a prominent place in the most beautiful square in
New England, save Copley square. It is a fit companion for its handsome neighbor, the post-office
and federal court house, and it lies almost in the
embrace of its foster parent, the state house.

The commission to which was entrusted the erection and furnishing of this building has discharged
its duties. How well, this handsome structure and
its no less handsome furniture tell. "Finis coronat
opus." In the language of our governor's inaugural, it is a "substantial and commodious structure;"
as "a work of art, instructive," and in "its strength
and durability a living prophecy of the perpetuity of
the institutions it shelters."

Still some modern "Momus" may carp at its architecture, or its arrangement, or cost.

To the thoughtful and patriotic citizen, such criticism will seem as unreasonable as that of his pro-
genitor, who found fault with Jupiter for not having
placed a window in the breast of man so that his
thoughts could be read. Were "Momus's lattice" in
the breasts of such carpers, their secret thoughts
would reveal the insincerity of their strictures.

If this building encounters such criticism, it will be exceptional and transitory. When the "chiefest temple" of all who are actors in the scenes of to-day, shall be a "tomb," and other eyes shall behold its substantial walls, and other voices awake the echoes of its lofty corridors, and other feet tread its mosaic walk, it will survive, a beautiful inspiration to wise thoughts and worthy deeds.

But, ladies and gentlemen, a wise man wrote,

"Let him be sure to leave other men their turns to speak."

Better things await you than I can offer, and without further introduction we will proceed with the dedicatory exercises.

INVOCATION BY REV. HARRY P. DEWEY.

Almighty God, we look to Thee for Thy blessing, as we enter upon the exercises of this hour, and we are humbly confident that Thou art pleased to hearken unto our prayer. We have come to dedicate this building. Thy hills and forests have furnished it substance; forces controlled by Thee hold its walls firm and strong; seeking to realize in its symmetry and grace the beautiful which Thou Who art altogether lovely, dost delight in, its designers and workmen have fashioned it; and all who have given or labored with brain or hand for its erection are Thy children ; but more than all must it be to Thee, that it is set apart to uses that are righteous and holy. We are grateful for the means and the skill and the toil which have made this imposing structure possible.

May its chaste and noble presence ever purify and elevate. May it be a persuasive sermon in stone to all who look upon it, reminding the citizen of the gracious ends it is appointed to serve, the ends of truth and justice. Our Father, may we who are assembled here feel that we are upon sacred ground. May every utterance of the lip and every thought of the heart be touched with a feeling of reverence as we reflect upon the high and exalted uses to which this edifice is consecrated. And in dedicating it, may we give ourselves to the cause of truth and justice, yea, to Thee, who art Perfect Truth, Perfect Justice. So shalt Thou be pleased to establish the works of our hands, and the house that is builded shall not have been raised up in vain. To Thee be praise and honor and dominion, now and evermore. Amen.

THE PRESIDENT.—We read in the Scriptures, " which of you intending to build a tower, sitteth not down first and counteth the cost, lest happly after he hath laid the foundation and is not able to finish, all that behold it begin to mock, saying, this man began to build and was not able to finish."

The commissioners entrusted with the erection and furnishing of this building, heeding the Scripture lesson, have counted the cost and finished. To-day they render it up to the state complete in all its appointments.

We come here to-day not to " mock," but to thank them.

Mr. Burns in behalf of the committee will now

deliver the keys to the governor, and the governor will respond without further announcement.

Presentation of the keys by Hon. Charles H. Burns :

Your Excellency:—The commissioners to whom was committed the duty of purchasing land and erecting thereon a suitable building for the accommodation of the supreme court and the State Library, have completed their work. It is now ready for inspection, dedication, and occupancy. It is hoped by the commissioners that it will be acceptable to the people of the state, and a blessing for many years.

This building has been designed and built for practical and useful purposes. While New Hampshire was the first state in the Union to empower towns "to maintain free public libraries by taxation" by a law enacted by its legislature almost half a century ago, and providing that such libraries should be "open to the free use of every inhabitant;" and while, under the impetus of this beneficent law, substantial library buildings have been erected and public libraries established and maintained throughout the state to the manifest advantage of our people, the state found itself in the possession of books, maps, charts, periodicals, and valuable documents of all sorts, increasing rapidly, and with no adequate rooms or safety vaults in which to keep them. It has been obliged to store large quantities in packages and boxes. In times past, books, papers, and manuscripts of great value and importance concerning colonial history, and which can now probably never be supplied, have been lost or destroyed for want of a place where they could be safely stored. This large and commodious room, with fireproof vaults, will furnish ample accommodations for our valuable library, of which we shall not be ashamed.

This building is to be the home of the supreme court. Here important questions concerning the rights of all the people are to be settled. It has not been creditable to the state that the court has never until now had a suitable place for its deliberations, and in which to hold its law sessions. Our citizens must be justly proud that the tribunal which is both their guide and guardian is now provided with comforts and conveniences to some extent commensurate with its manifest necessities, and with its high character and usefulness.

This substantial building, erected by the state, aided materially by the city of Concord in the gift of a valuable tract of land, supplies these wants in a manner befitting the dignity and honor of the commonwealth. The prosperity of a state does not depend upon the beauty or convenience of its public buildings, but, rather, upon its men and women of culture, character, and conscience; but such buildings do contribute in large measure to the cultivation of the tastes of its people, inspiring them with grander ideals of strength and beauty. This noble edifice of ours is to be filled with books containing the best thoughts of the great thinkers of all ages, and with "whatsoever things are lovely, whatsoever things are pure," in art; it is to be the home of the highest court of the commonwealth, where justice—

2

whose seat, like law, is "the bosom of God"—shall be dispensed; and it will become an indispensable source of protection, enlightenment, and education to our citizens, raising higher and still higher the standards of civilization;—for law and learning go hand in hand, and are the most effective of human instrumentalities in the structure and superintendence of society.

It is, therefore, with pride and satisfaction that, in behalf of my associates and myself, I deliver to you, as the custodian of the property of the state, the key to this beautiful building.

Response by His Excellency Charles A. Busiel:

In behalf of the State of New Hampshire, I accept from your hand the key to the new state library. In the discharge of an agreeable duty I am permitted to express my appreciation of the ability and the success of the commissioners who have formulated the plans and have directed the construction of this elegant and commodious building.

Your labors, in this direction, are happily ended. The completed building in all its appointments reflects your wisdom and your ready appreciation of the needs of the present and the demands of the future.

I congratulate the trustees and the patrons of the library, and the judges and officers of the supreme court, on the completion of this commodious structure.

By a thoughtful impulse the people have liberally provided for the future accommodation of the library and of the court.

As we proceed with the services of dedication, the inspiration of the day should be an invitation to renewed labor and enlarged usefulness on the part of all who are the chosen tenants and custodians of this spacious and attractive temple.

THE PRESIDENT:—A portion of this building has been set aside for the use of the supreme court. The appointments of the court room are so elegant, that it is not impossible, that you, gentlemen of the legislature, may be called upon to make an appropriation to purchase silken gowns for the members of the court, that their personal adornments may comport with those of the room. It was hoped that the Chief Justice might so favor this judicial embellishment, that he would be present to-day; but with characteristic modesty, he has deputed Judge Smith to represent the court.

Judge Smith, to the regret of all, is soon to retire from the place he has so long adorned. I know you will all listen with interest to what may be his last public judicial utterance.

Judge Isaac W. Smith responded as follows:

Our congratulations are due to the distinguished gentlemen of the building committee for the success which has crowned their labors. This spacious building, beautiful in design, in construction, and in finish, is a lasting monument of their united wisdom. We cheerfully acknowledge the estimable value of their services to the State in the discharge of the varied and, perhaps at times, perplexing duties

imposed upon them by the legislature. Their success lies not in the fact alone that here is a building
beautiful in its architectural effect, which the eye
views with delight and the mind dwells upon with
pleasure,—but also a building solid as the native
granite of which its walls are built, massive in its
structure, and planned in its minutest details for the
imperative wants and necessities of the State. Their
reward consists in the conscious knowledge that the
service so cheerfully rendered is fully appreciated by
a grateful people.

The state is also to be congratulated, that at
length, after much patient waiting, and after no little
inconvenience from unsuitable, and overcrowded
apartments, it has come into possession of a building
so admirably adapted to the purposes of its construction. The people, through the legislature, have
brought hither their offerings for its erection, that
they may enjoy accommodations so imperatively required by their growing wants and increased prosperity. Without lavish expenditures of money, they
have provided a building worthy the dignity of the
state, and the intelligence of its people, and in keep-
ing with their simple tastes and frugal habits ; where
there is " comfort without luxury, and elegance without display."

Wilberforce said, in the British House of Com-
mons, "Wherever the English language is spoken,
men shall be free." He meant the freedom that
comes from minds enlightened by knowledge, and
from hearts inspired by the love of justice. The
framers of our constitution, recognizing this truth,

inserted in the fundamental law of the state this, as article 82: " Knowledge and learning generally diffused through a community being essential to the preservation of a free government, and spreading the opportunities and advantages of education through the various parts of the country being highly conducive to promote this end, it shall be the duty of the legislators and magistrates . . . to cherish the interest of literature and the sciences, and all seminaries and public schools," etc. The sources of knowledge are many and illimitable: the family, the common school from lowest to higher grades, the academy, college, seminary, pulpit, press, stump, and, what interests us at this present moment, the library, the power of which no man can weigh or describe. It is sometimes called the "People's University." Within these alcoves will be deposited for use of the historian, the scholar, the bibliographer,— of every one in search of facts, or thirsting for knowledge, forty thousand books and pamphlets,— the slow accretion of a century, upon law, theology, medicine, science, and the arts. The suggestion of His Excellency, the Governor, in his message to the legislature of last week, whether some system of administration may not be found which shall render its usefulness more general, is deserving of the fullest consideration, the discussion of which I leave to those better qualified by study and experience.

I am invited to speak in behalf of my brethren in acceptance of the apartments provided in this structure, and this day dedicated to the use and accommodation of the supreme court of the state.

We turn instinctively to the names of our judges whose lives have passed into history. The occasion does not require nor permit a biographical sketch of their lives, nor even a review of their judicial work, were I able to perform that interesting duty. A brief insight into the times in which they lived, and the environment by which they were surrounded, is all that is permissible on this occasion.

In colonial times the practice prevailed of making judges of men who were not lawyers. It is said that this practice was general in New England. Paul Dudley, appointed in 1718, is said to have been the first person regularly bred to the law, who sat on the bench in Massachusetts. Of Richard Martyn, chief-justice of New Hampshire in 1693, 1694, the late Governor Bell, in his valuable "History of the Bench and Bar of New Hampshire," says, "He appears to have possessed intelligence and good business qualifications, and to have performed his public trusts acceptibly;" of William Vaughn, chief-justice in 1708–1716, "He was an honest and courageous supporter of the people's rights and interests, and was the object of their warm affection and admiration;" of Samuel Penhallow, justice in 1714–1717, and chief-justice in 1717–1726, "His mental powers, his education, and his familiarity with public business rendered him a valuable and excellent judge;" of George Jaffrey, justice in 1717–1726, and chief-justice in 1726–1732, a graduate of Harvard college in 1702, "He was the first man of liberal education who appeared on the bench in New Hampshire. . . . . His long service in public offices indicates the confidence he inspired in his ability and integrity;" of Nicholas Gilman, justice from 1732–1740, "He performed the duties satisfactorily;" of Benjamin Gambling, justice in 1733–1737, that he was characterized by Governor Belcher as "knowing and honest;" of Samuel Gilman, justice in 1740–1747, "He was a man of the highest character, and universally respected;" of Meshech Weare, justice in 1747–1775, chief-justice in 1776–1782, "During the Revolution he administered simultaneously the highest offices in the state, legislative, judicial, and executive,—a conjunction of powers which, under the circumstances, and in a man of less principle and patriotism, would have been hazardous in the extreme. . . . . He sat thirty-five years upon the bench of the superior court, where his father and grandfather had sat before him,—a remarkable succession never paralleled;" of William Parker, justice in 1771–1775, "By common consent allowed to be at the head of his profession in New Hampshire;" of John Wentworth, justice in 1776–1781, "a man of intelligent views, and a sincere patriot;" of Josiah Bartlett, justice in 1782–1790, and chief-justice in 1790, physician, delegate to the Continental congress, signer of the Declaration of Independence, and president and governor of New Hampshire three years, "His fellow citizens reposed in his honesty and ability, and he executed the duties of his important stations with general approbation."

The Revolution, it will be seen, brought with it new men. Of Samuel Livermore, chief-justice in

1782–1790, William Plumer, Jr., in his scholarly tribute in memory of his father, published in 1856, says: "Though bred to the law, he was not inclined to attach much importance to precedents, or to any merely systematic or technical rules of procedure. In a manuscript report which I have of one of his charges," writes Mr. Plumer, "I find him cautioning the jury against paying too much attention to the niceties of the law, to the prejudice of justice—a caution of which juries do not ordinarily stand much in need."

John Dudley, justice in 1785–1797, was a trader and farmer. Woodbury Langdon, justice in 1782–1791, was a merchant of Portsmouth. Timothy Farrar of New Ipswich, justice in 1791–1803, was originally designed for the pulpit. Of them Plumer says: "These judges were men of strong powers of mind, of large acquaintance with business, and superior in talents and information generally to second rate lawyers." Jeremiah Smith, in 1796, wrote,—"There are now two lawyers on the bench, but I think they are by no means the two best of the four. Farrar and Dudley, in my judgment, greatly overmatch them." Theophilus Parsons of Massachusetts, who practised many years in our courts, and later was chief-justice of that state, said of Dudley,— "You may laugh at his law, and ridicule his language, but Dudley is, after all, the best judge I ever knew in New Hampshire." Arthur Livermore said that "justice was never better administered in New Hampshire than when the judges knew very little of what we lawyers call law." Plumer writes that Webster told him he had heard the story that a question on demurrer filed by Mason was put by Dudley to the jury. Happy the judge who could thus rid himself of the decision of a troublesome question of law, and retain the respect of such men as Parsons and Jeremiah Smith.

The consensus of opinion is that substantial justice was done in the determination of questions involving the property, rights, and liberties of the people; and our admiration is increased when we consider that the bench and bar of the seventeenth and eighteenth centuries had almost no books on legal subjects. When William Plumer in 1785 entered the office of John Prentice in Londonderry (afterwards attorney-general) his law library consisted of Blackstone's Commentaries, Wood's Institutes of the Laws of England, Hawkins' Pleas of the Crown, Jacobs' Law Dictionary, Salkeld, Raymond and Strange's Reports, the New Hampshire Statutes, and a manuscript volume of pleas and declarations. The year previous in the office of Joshua Atherton in Amherst he was given Coke upon Littleton as his first initiation into the mysteries of the law. Plumer (Jr.) is authority for the statement that when Patrick Henry applied for admission to the Virginia bar, he was asked by Jefferson what books he had read, and replied with entire confidence in the extent of his legal acquirements, Coke upon Littleton and the Virginia Statutes.

Lord Campbell says that "In the simple and happy times of Edward I, Glanville, Bracton, and Fleta composed a complete law library." Plumer, writing between

1850 and 1854, estimates the number of reports of law courts then in existence as between 500 and 1,000. To-day they are estimated at 4,000.   In this paucity of books, judges as well as lawyers looked for the law as deduced from acknowledged legal principles. From necessity, they dealt less with authorities and more with the reason of the law, and attempted to find the rule in the immutable principles of justice.

The nineteenth century brought with it as judges men of judicial science. Of Jeremiah Smith, chief-justice in 1802–1809, and in 1813–1816, Bell says he "did more perhaps for the improvement of the state than any other man.   Like the monarch who changed a city from brick to marble, he found law without form and void, and during his connection with the courts he reduced it to order and harmony.   His genius was constructive; he had the systematizing faculty.   He did not conceive of the law as a mass of detached, independent rules; in his mind it was a series of requirements, each connected with and deducible from great central principles.   Before his day the judges were mostly unversed in the technique of the law, and aimed at what they deemed to be equitable conclusions.   The result was that no man could foresee with any confidence the issue of any cause. Judge Smith drew straight the lines which had been confused or obliterated, and gave the bar and the public firm ground on which to stand.   The counsel who knew the law began to take his place above the mere tonguy man who saw nothing beyond the case in hand.   The influence of this upon the bar and upon the administration of reme-

dial justice could not fail to be of the most benefi-
cial character. Fortunately we have now the evidence of Judge Smith's reformatory work in a durable form. A volume of his decisions from his own
manuscript has been recently published, which bears
unmistakable testimony to his vigorous and scientific
administration of the law. . . . It was unfortu-
nate that it was withheld so long, for if the opinions
contained in it had been at once promulgated, great
expense would have been saved to parties who sub-
sequently litigated the very questions which Judge
Smith had before settled so conclusively."

The state was equally fortunate in the selection of
his successor, William M. Richardson, chief-justice
from 1816 to his decease in 1838. With his induc-
tion into office was commenced the publication of
reports of cases adjudicated in the superior court.
His opinion in the famous Dartmouth College case,
although overruled by the supreme court of the
United States, has always been regarded as one of
the ablest on that side of the question litigated.
Bell says of him, "The judicial ermine received no
stain from his wearing it. He knew no friends and
no enemies while in the seat of judgment, nor any
of the ordinary lines of decisions among men. His
ideal was the very highest." Judge Perley in " East-
man v. Meredith, 36 N. H., 284, 299," speaks of him
as "our own learned and excellent Chief-Justice
Richardson" in connection with Parsons and Shaw
of Massachusetts and Mellen and Shepley of Maine,
" names which carry with them an irresistible weight
of authority on all legal questions."

The memory of Joel Parker, justice in 1833–1838, and chief-justice in 1838–1848, is yet green with the present generation of lawyers. In ability and learning he was fully the equal of his two distinguished predecessors. His published opinions in thirteen volumes of the New Hampshire Reports show his familiarity both with the authorities and with fundamental legal principles, and established our reports as high legal authority with his cotemporaries. Smith, Richardson, and Parker formed a trio " of the most able and learned of a sequence of jurists rarely equalled in the annals of any state."

Time forbids more than allusion to their successors: Gilchrist, scholarly, industrious, popular; Woods, even-tempered, patient, and upright; Perley, strong, positive, self-reliant, *primus inter pares*, whose opinions in style and substance are unsurpassed in our reports; Bell, clear-headed, strong-minded, *justum et tenacem propositi virum*; Bellows, the high-minded, gracious gentleman and learned and conscientious judge; Sargent, careful, painstaking, and sensible; and Cushing, the polished gentleman and scholar, and patient and learned jurist; these were the magistrates to whom with their learned associates New Hampshire entrusted the enforcement of her laws, and whose memories we gratefully cherish.

Five times within the century, in the mad passion engendered of political strife, has the court been overturned. That this action of the legislative department was acquiesced in does not render it any the less deplorable or questionable. It may be per-

mitted, perhaps, to one who looks forward with a
sense of relief from official responsibility to the early
day when he shall again put on the gown of the bar,
to express the hope that henceforth better counsels
will prevail, and the line of separation between the
legislative and judicial departments of the government marked out in the fundamental law of the state
be kept intact.

The chief-justice in 1905 will probably write no
better opinions, seated in his upholstered chair at his
table of quartered oak in yonder spacious and commodious rooms embellished by art, than did his
predecessor, Chief-Justice Bell in 1860, seated in
his plain chair before his table of pine.   For the
principles of justice are immutable ; but its growing
spirit inspires the world.   Wendell Phillips said that
to be as good as our fathers we must be better.   We
cannot cast any dishonor on our fathers; but we
shall honor them best by taking what is best and
not by being content with their limitations.   Discon-
tent no less than contentment may be a virtue.
To-day is not as yesterday.   It is not a good thing
to think one's work cannot be better done, because
it can be better done.   There may be great truths
in law and ethics as in the arts and sciences
not yet attained.   Therefore as we this day conse-
crate this beautiful temple to the cause of learning
and justice, may the memories which cluster around
the past incite us and our successors to higher
achievements in the cause of good government, that
this structure in all that it stands for in the pro-
motion of law, order, and knowledge be endeared

in the hearts of the people as long as it shall stand.

THE PRESIDENT:—I believe the whole state (excepting possibly Manchester) is disposed to credit the capital city with a generous act in the donation of a part of the land occupied in connection with this building.

Mayor Cogswell, in behalf of the city of Concord, will make to you such suggestions as may seem to him pertinent in regard to his city's connection with the selection and purchase of the site of this building.

RESPONSE OF HON. P. B. COGSWELL, MAYOR OF CONCORD.

As a representative of the municipal government of the capital city, it gives me pleasure to assist in the dedication of this superb edifice to the noble purposes for which it is designed. In a spirit befitting part of the motto of our city seal—" Law, Education"—the city council responded to the call of the state library commissioners for additional land to enable them to carry out more completely their plans for this library building, by condemning in the spring of 1892, certain real estate on the north, extending to Centre street. The awarded damages to the owners of that property aggregated over $25,000, and provision for payment thereof was made by a temporary loan, which was met by the present city council authorizing an issue of bonds bearing three and one half per cent. interest. It is a fact which may possess some historical interest hereafter, that these are the lowest rate interest-bearing bonds ever issued by any city or town of our good old commonwealth, and that most of them were taken by our own citizens.

When the library commissioners called last spring for the land taken for a public park, the city council ordered the speedy removal of the houses situated thereon, and aided in the construction of substantial sidewalks on the streets around this building and its grounds. The city of Concord has thus met all the calls made upon it by the state library commissioners concerning this edifice, and faithfully fulfilled all of its obligations relating thereto. I confess to a feeling akin to pride for our goodly city in that it has borne its part so well in furthering the aim of the commissioners to provide a befitting home for our state library, and suitable apartments for the administration of justice, guarded by law.

Of the helpfulness and unmeasurable usefulness of public libraries, it is not my province to speak. Others who have profited from them, largely and wisely, will hold your attention with apt and gracious words concerning them. It only remains for me to commend the state library commissioners for the able, faithful, and successful manner in which they have discharged the duties imposed upon them by the legislature of 1891; and to congratulate the trustees of the state library and all its beneficiaries, and the Supreme Court of our state, that they are to have so beautiful, commodious, and well-appointed quarters in the future as this edifice of enduring granite and marble will afford them. I am sure I voice the sentiment of all present in expressing the hope that this building may long escape the crumbling decay incident to age and climate, and that the state library to be housed herein may never suffer from fire, or flood, or other destructive agency, but that it may continue to grow in interest and value to our city and state for centuries to come, aye, "to the last syllable of recorded time."

THE PRESIDENT:—From this day the active management and control of this library will be assumed by its trustees.

The present board is eminently well qualified for the proper discharge of this important duty, and we only hope that in the coming years its interests will always find as intelligent and faithful guardians as those who are to-day represented by their president, whom I now have the pleasure of introducing to you,—Mr. Gilmore of Manchester.

REMARKS BY HON. GEORGE C. GILMORE IN BEHALF OF THE TRUSTEES OF THE STATE LIBRARY.

Little, I apprehend, is expected of the local management in the exercises of to-day, our duties being all of the future, and it would certainly be presumption on my part to attempt to interest this large audience by anything I might say, especially so when our distinguished guests are waiting on the platform to be heard,—men who have given a life time to library management. But I cannot forbear saying a few words to place on record the early efforts of the inhabitants of the towns in this state to establish libraries. Dover is undoubtedly entitled to the honor of having been the first in the list, as

early as July, 1776, although the charter for her
social library was not granted until December 18,
1792; Rochester's social library chartered February
14, 1794; Portsmouth's and Tamworth's both the
same date, June 14, 1796, the above being the first
four charters granted; from 1792 to 1800, sixty, and
from 1801 to 1883, one hundred and eighty-seven,
making a total of two hundred and forty-seven, and
at the present time only sixty towns are without a
library.

The petitioners for the social library of Tamworth
present the advantages of a library as follows:
"Whereas a general diffusion of useful knowledge
in a land of liberty has a happy tendency to preserve freedom, and make better men and better
citizens."

The first absolutely free public library is supposed
to be that of the town of Peterborough, in 1833.
The legislature of New Hampshire in July, 1849,
passed an act allowing towns to maintain libraries
by taxation, being the first act authorizing the
people of the several towns to tax themselves to
maintain libraries, in the United States.

THE PRESIDENT:—Without any disloyalty to our
own *alma mater*, we all have a feeling of pride in
our state institution of learning, which is now having
a new birth under its recently appointed president,—
a man known and honored by scholars all over the
land.

I think I may adopt the words of the brilliant
English essayist and historian, in introducing to you

Rev. Dr. Tucker, president of Dartmouth College,
"He is a man of the world among men of letters,
and a man of letters among men of the world."

MR. CHAIRMAN, YOUR EXCELLENCY, YOUR HONORS,
AND GENTLEMEN OF THE LEGISLATURE: I ask at once
in your presence,—the question is prompted by the
occasion,—how shall we ensure to the state or
commonwealth, a rightful part in the present revival
of civic pride throughout the country?

The chief effect of that revival, as we are now
conscious of it, is the glorious assurance of nationality. "We the people" have at last become the
nation, and we know it. It has not been an easy
matter for us to reach this supreme consciousness.
As late as 1811 Josiah Quincy made this confession
from his seat in congress: " Sir, I confess it, the first
public love of my heart is the Commonwealth of
Massachusetts. There is my fireside; there are the
tombs of my ancestors." That was the utterance,
not of South Carolina, but of Massachusetts, in the
national house of representatives, twenty-three years
after the adoption of the constitution. No Massachusetts man, no man, I trust, from any state, would
utter that sentiment now. The events of our generation, in which some of you were actors, have
wrought a mighty change in our opinions and in our
feelings. The nation sits enthroned to-day in the
hearts of the people. The most interesting and the
most inspiring expression of civic pride is this calm
but proud consciousness of nationality. We are
beginning to realize to ourselves the great conception

of Milton : " Not many sovereignties united in one commonwealth, but many commonwealths in one united and entrusted sovereignty."

The present revival of civic pride may be seen at work, if not equally, yet with marked effect, at the other extreme of our political organization, in the municipality. Next to the national feeling, the municipal feeling is at present the strongest. Something of this feeling is due of course to the recognized peril of the cities. It is in many cases the sense of danger which tests the depth of our affection, which may discover the fact itself to us. Probably no city in the country has had, in proportion to its importance, less municipal pride than the city of New York, but he must be less than an alien, whether resident for longer or shorter time, who does not now feel the responsibility of citizenship The sense of responsibility, however, is not the chief sign of municipal pride, but rather the increasing sense of opportunity. The city is beginning to stand for more than size ; it represents every possible advance and improvement. The period of silly rivalries and competitions about numbers has been out-grown, and account is being taken of solid and substantial growths. Men are seeking to be identified not only in personal interest, but in reputation and name with their respective cities. Schools, libraries, museums, parks, bearing the names of individual donors, are the visible evidence of an enlarged municipal enthusiasm ; while the surer though less conspicuous sign is found in the fact that here and there a citizen of acknowledged capacity is willing to forego further gains in his business or profession, that he may answer in person the demand for honest and capable government. The ardent imagination of Mr. Depew interprets a popular tendency, when he predicts that the second office in the United States will soon be that of mayor of greater New York.

Now in this revival of civic pride, so manifestly affecting the nation and the city, what of the state, the old commonwealth, the original substance and life out of which in due time the nation was born, and from whose permanent and abounding vitality cities are now springing forth? Evidently the day for the reassertion of rights once surrendered is forever past, and no encroachment upon the interests of the growing communities may be allowed. But the commonwealth remains, worthy of a like place in the honorable pride of its citizens with that held by the nation or a city.

And amongst us the opportunity, if not the necessity, for some very practical expression of this pride of state, is apparent in the fact that the influence of New Hampshire is not overshadowed by that of a great municipality within its borders. With us the state is not in bondage to the city, nor subordinate to it. Neither can the state throw off its responsibility to provide for the higher wants of its citizens upon any one locality, equipped with all the modern appliances of progress,—the library, the museum, the university. In few states of the nation are the resources so variously, if not equally, distributed as in our own. Every section of it, east and west, south and north, has a share in its history. The whole state had its pre-existence in the province. And under the incoming of the later industries, and the consequent re-distribution of population, the ancient equality has not been altogether destroyed. It is the state, not a city, which still offers the great attraction to visitors from far and near. It is the state, not any one locality, which holds undeveloped resources out of which new industries may spring for the support of new populations. It is the state at large which shelters the great schools, which send out the sons of New Hampshire into other states, and which draw to their training the sons of all the states. It is, in a word, the state, the old commonwealth in its entirety, not a city, not any localized centre, by means of which we are to maintain the honor of our inheritance, and keep step with the march of the nation.

I welcome therefore, Mr. Chairman, as a citizen of New Hampshire, the occasion in which we dedicate in the name of the state another building, the choicest of its outward possessions, to be henceforth one more visible reminder of the real presence and personality of the commonwealth. I rejoice especially in the object of this building, which shows in so representative a way the enlarging functions of the state. It answers in part, by illustration at least, the question with which I began—how shall we ensure to the commonwealth its share in the present revival of civic pride?

I go on then to speak of the maintenance of the state library as one of the means through which we may show our pride of state, and also as one of the agencies through which we may develop the higher interests of the commonwealth. I congratulate myself and you that I may restrict my further thought to this nearer aspect of the present occasion in view of the scope of the address which is to follow. It is to the honor of New Hampshire that at the dedication of its library building, the state may summon one of its sons from his post at the head of the national library.

It may seem almost too obvious for me to say, that it is through the agency of the library, that the state is best able to avail itself of its own history. But the full meaning of this statement does not appear in the utterance of it. The history of a great past is made available only to the degree in which it can be reproduced in spirit in the continuous life of a people. But what is the continuous life of a people? What is the continuous life of the people of New Hampshire? Not the unbroken succession of families. Not the local increase of the native stock. Names once significant in the annals of the state have disappeared, or appear only in remoter regions. Families of wide connection and of extended influence remain as remnants. Others, let us rejoice, survive in the fullness of their strength, and gain upon their heritage. But if the state, if any of the older states, were dependent upon the original stock it would exist as a fragment of its former self, unless it could call home its own. The state continues to live through the incoming of the new, through constant accessions from various and

unforeseen sources. This continuity of life is absolutely dependent upon the process of assimilation,
the moral part of which lies in the power of the state
to impress its principles, its history, itself, upon
those who may choose to share its fortunes.

Pardon me if I pause to assert and emphasize the
fact, that there are none amongst us upon whom the
great men and the great events of our history are
making a deeper impression, than upon the more
receptive minds of the new population. We ignore
or underestimate this fact in times of social depres-
sion. We forget the philosophy which underlies it.
Noble traditions lose their power when held in too
easy and familiar possession. Inspiration does not
long abide in what has become to anyone the com-
monplace. But the familiar deed springs into new-
ness of life as often as it gains a fresh hearing. It
is not alone the new seed, it is the new soil, which
explains the harvest. Again and again have I
watched the kindling of eager minds, coming from
other states, as I have told the early story of Dartmouth, that heroic romance in education, when there
was nothing in personal inheritance or personal
association to waken the mind, nothing but the
contact of an inspiring history with a quick intelligence. We grievously mistake if we suppose that
history appeals only to those who are the natural
heirs to the deeds which it records. History never
fails in its appeal to men as they come and go, provided the sources are kept full and open, so that it
may be rewritten to the mind of each generation.
Here is the advantage in part of such a library as

this, in distinction from the ordinary private, educational, or public library. We build here upon foundations already laid a great storehouse for originals—documents of every sort illustrative of early and later history, dispatches, records, reports, addresses, letters,—nothing of this nature too small or too remote to be neglected. This is not the material for a circulating library. It has another use and another value. Here is the material on deposit which gives worth to the current literature of its kind. You open here a home and a workshop for the investigator, the scholar, the writer, the man who is to come hither with knowledge and imagination, capable of translating this ancient life into the speech and life of to-day. So you make the history of the state available in ever recurring variety of form. For, as I have intimated, it is of the very genius of history, that it should be written to an age, and therefore its story continually retold with new motive and in new setting. The age which sings the Iliad to the notes of camp and battle and siege, is not content till it has sung the Odyssey in the strains of love and home and kindred, the arts of peace, and the common ways of men. Every considerable period of history presents various aspects. We want to know them all to know the period. We want to know, of course, the story of discovery, and adventure, and war; we want to know the record of political struggle, and religious advance, and educational development, the growth of the arts and industries. There is the true source and reason of events, the mere narration of which we sometimes think makes history. History in its highest form is the discovery of cause and reason ; it is the explanation of actions and events. We read the memorable speech of the "Defender of the Constitution" through which he postponed secession for thirty years, and made it thereafter more possible to save the Union. Is that speech of Mr. Webster's to be explained by its own greatness? Not at all. His father had made it before him. At that critical hour when the convention of New Hampshire met to adopt or reject the constitution, when its vote to adopt would complete the number of states necessary to form the Union, when the conventions of New York and Virginia then in session were anxiously waiting the result, couriers having been stationed by order of Hamilton to carry the news from Concord to Poughkeepsie, and on to Richmond, in that convention where the result was in serious doubt, Colonel Webster arose and uttered this sentiment,—the language may show the revision of a later hand:

"Mr. President : I have listened to the arguments for and against the constitution. I am convinced that such a government as that constitution will establish, if adopted—a government acting directly on the people of the states—is necessary for the common defense and the general welfare. It is the only government which will enable us to pay the national debt, the debt which we owe for the Revolution, and which we are bound in honor fully and fairly to discharge. Sir, I shall vote for its adoption."

The reply to Hayne was the echo of the speech of the New Hampshire farmer. It was the same spirit which urged the adoption of the constitution in that hour of doubt, which, in the hour of its danger, rose to its defense. The speech was in the blood.

The constant and honorable boast of New Hampshire has been of the quality of the men whom she could furnish to the nation. One historian writes of a given administration, and that one of the best, that at its time New Hampshire could have furnished from the number of her own public men, the full equivalent for those who held the offices of president and vice-president, and also of those who held seats in the cabinet. Grant it. Who were behind these men, and made them possible? As we have seen in an illustrious instance, such men do not explain themselves. You might as well try to explain the flow of the Merrimack as it sweeps these meadows on its way to the struggle and toil below, without pointing to the hills, as to attempt to explain the public men of the state without going back into the life of the people. What we ask, therefore, first of all for this library, is that it shall be made complete to the last degree in whatever pertains to the history of the people of the state ; that it shall be a repository, not only for public documents, but also for private papers ; that it shall reach out after all facts, however transmitted, which have a bearing on vital questions of state interest ; and that it shall be able to trace the great events in which the state has had a part, and the great men whom it has sent forth, back to the causes which determined or produced them. What we want, in a word, is a library which will *explain* New Hampshire.

A more direct, if not equally obvious, use of the library for the advancement of the state, is to be seen in the very great aid which it offers toward intelligent legislation, the interpretation of the laws and general administration. Doubtless we have in this use of the library the chief intent of its founders. The statute under which the library is administered, provides first that it shall be "for the use of the governor and council, officers of the state government, the legislature and the clerks thereof, the judges of the supreme court, and such other persons as the trustees may determine;" and afterward in fixing the duties of the trustees, it prescribes that "they shall procure for the library full sets of the statutes and law reports of the United States, and of the several states; histories, including those of the counties and towns of the state whenever published; maps, charts, works on agriculture, political economy, the arts and natural sciences, copies of state papers and publications relating to the material, social, and religious conditions of the people, or bearing upon the business and objects of legislation, and such other works as they may deem suitable, works of fiction excepted."

Naturally this is a law library in its largest intent and purpose. The provision which has been made in this building for the sessions of the supreme court emphasizes this purpose, as also the mention of the duty, first among those prescribed for the trustees, "of procuring for the library full sets of

the statutes and law reports of the United States
and of the several states." It is a matter of congrat-
ulation, that in the comparison which this array of
statutes and reports invites, the reports of New
Hampshire hold by common consent so high and
honorable a place. Indeed this was to have been
expected, if we recall the names, which, in the
quaint language of a former generation, "reflected
the gladsome light of jurisprudence,"—the names of
Weare, Bartlett, Langdon, Livermore, Woodbury,
Bell, Smith, Parker, Perley, and so many of their
associates,—an honor one and all to any bench.

It does not fall to my lot to speak of the relation
of the state to its bench or courts, but without
venturing beyond the province of a layman, I may
fitly call attention to the present demand for the
more general knowledge of what may be termed the
literature of the law, the knowledge of statutes and
reports, as indispensable to wise legislation. As
any one can see, the relation between the federal
and state authority is becoming at certain points
complicated and sensitive. No past political conditions have ever involved issues of greater perplexity
than those involved in present economic and industrial conditions. Decisions are rendered almost
every month by some one of the United States
courts affecting the interests of corporations and of
labor in every state of the Union. Not long since,
in a western state, I chanced to listen to an after-
dinner speech from one of the younger judges of
the United States court of appeals, in which, though
a man of remarkable wit, he put aside at once the

pleasantries of the hour that he might impress upon the company the very great seriousness of the questions upon which the federal courts were called upon to pass in determining the rights of property and the rights of service. The discussion was as earnest as an utterance of the pulpit. And between the states the lack of uniformity in the very principles of legislation is becoming in some cases not only serious but grievous. One has but to refer in illustration to subjects so widely removed from one another as taxation and divorce. At such a time the value of a state library which gives ready and complete information on all points of current decisions and statute law cannot be overestimated. A library with these facilities seems as much a part of the equipment of the legislature as of the courts. It has a distinct moral influence. Through its system of exchange it keeps open communication between the states. It enables us to realize the closeness of the fellowship of the body politic. " If one member suffers, all the members suffer with it."

The statute, however, which wisely gives precedence to law in the furnishing of the library, makes generous provision for other subjects which have to do with the material and social development of the state. I see no reason why this provision should not be fulfilled, as far as the annual appropriations may allow. The teachers of the state have already asked that a department of pedagogy may be opened. Why should not requests be urged from other sources? Why, for example, should not the library be made tributary to our great industries?

Where should one interested in any one of these
expect to look for careful information except to such
a library as this? Where else within the state could
one hope to find it? Technical departments are to
be found to a certain extent in our educational
libraries, and here and there the public library of a
city may provide some books of this character on a
given industry. But to what source ought one to
turn for such discriminating and well-directed information on the industries of the state as to the
state library? Here again I must remind you that we
have no great centre to which we can look except to
the state itself. And in so far as the state may see
fit to answer this demand, let us suggest that whenever any department of this kind is set up, the fact
be made known, and a classified list of the books in
the department be published and circulated. Grad-
ually and without undue expense, the state library
may become an authority upon many matters of
industrial and economic value.

Allow me the further suggestion that such works
as have to do most immediately with the resources
of the state be duplicated, and distributed at convenient centres, usually in connection with a town
library, but under the control of the state library.
Such a distribution would create among our citizens
a habit of thinking about the state and its interests.
It would provide material in advance for our legisla-
tures. It would add to that general intelligence
which they bring to their duties a special knowledge
on many points, which there is little time to gain
during the session of the legislature. It would be a

step for the state to take out among the people, arousing them to a greater interest in their citizenship. Like the attempt of which I have spoken to make the library available for recovering the history of the state, it would make the library more available for its present and future advancement. A great library, of any kind whatever, is more than a repository. That is its second use. The first and supreme object is to inform, incite, awaken. Rightly used, it is one of the creative agencies of civilization.

Assuming that the specific uses of a state library are such as have been indicated, namely, to give the state the advantage among its citizens of its own history, and to aid the state appropriately in the making and interpretation of its laws, and the development of its resources, it remains for me to speak of the library as standing for the identification of the state with the whole intellectual life of the people. In the language of the inaugural address, "its relations to our educational system should be intimate." I take the apt suggestion of the term. Intimacy of relationship rather than domination or control is the characteristic of the New England states in their educational policy. The distinction in educational policy between the earlier and later commonwealths is marked. The later commonwealths, almost without exception, have created elaborate educational systems, culminating in a university, which they support and control. The earlier commonwealths demand popular education as the basis of citizenship, and within certain limits they carefully provide for it, but they seek to arouse the public spirit of indi-

vidual citizens, and to develop private munificence.
Hence the peculiar phenomena, to be seen on every
hand, attending the intellectual development of New
England; great schools, colleges, and universities
founded and maintained by endowments; the fortunes of private citizens returning in part to their
native towns in the gift of libraries; voluntary associations springing up in all parts of the community
for the mutual advantage and improvement of their
members. Meanwhile the state is no mere on-
looker, an indifferent or curious spectator, its interests elsewhere, itself intent on other and lower ends.
The state is the watchful guardian, the solicitous
friend, the helper and patron. Its interest in whatever concerns the intellectual life of the people is
active, constant, and altogether beneficent. The
state acts by various methods; now working through
legislation, as when it reaffirms more vigorously the
principle of compulsory intelligence; now entering
into coöperation with the communities under its
care, as in the library system of our own state and
of Massachusetts; now granting immunities and
privileges to institutions of learning when necessary
to their freedom, not hesitating if need be to offer
the helping hand; and now teaching by example, as
by this occasion, and through the dignity and worth
of its own standards, broadening the public thought,
and elevating the public taste. Such by tradition
and by increasing practice, is the New England commonwealth in the intimacy of its relationship to the
intellectual life of the people. It was a statesman,
you recall, not a theorist, a mere scholar or poet,

who said, "The state is a partnership in all science, a partnership in all art, a partnership in every virtue. And as the end of such a partnership cannot be obtained in many generations, it becomes a partnership not only between those who are living, but between those who are living, and those who are dead, and those who are yet to be born."

It is impossible to overestimate the impression which the state is able to make upon its citizens through this noble union, this high partnership in great interests. Nothing else can rouse them to such a degree of civic pride.

The state, we must remember, does not always appear before us in this aspect. So many of its functions are negative and repressive. It is through the state that we deal with crime. Much of its legislation is the iteration of the commandments. There is a majesty in this aspect of the state, and there is benignity. The other side of law is security, order, peace. Still it is not through its repressive force that we respond most heartily to the power of the state.

Through other functions the state is concerned chiefly with material interests. These interests are vital. Nothing concerns any man more than his daily work, the work itself, and the result of it in his livelihood. But the actual power of the state to affect business is far less than that of the general government. In every state election the issue broadens into the field of national politics. No citizen looks exclusively to his own commonwealth for the adjustment of those conditions which determine his work, his business, or his investments.

The state is excluded from the province of religion. The experiment once tried in that direction will never be repeated. The one reservation which the individual citizen has made for himself for all time is liberty of conscience, in every possible expression of it, and in all its results.

The open field into which the state may enter, where it may exercise unhindered its higher ministry, where it may illustrate this noble partnership, is education, the development of the intellectual, and through that, the moral life of the people. The essential contribution of New Hampshire, as we fondly believe, to the life of the nation, has been mental character, not simply brain power, not simply conscience, but character informed and developed by the trained mind. That has been the ground of our boasting. We have no other to compare with it. It can have no equivalent and no substitute. We may cherish local associations in the state with a sentiment which will idealize even its rugged and barren hills. We may respect the authority of the state as it guards our rights, and protects our interests. But the one source of civic pride for the state is the maintenance of its extraordinary intellectual and moral history. It is the remembrance of that, and that above all else, which quickens the blood, and stirs the spirit within us.

Fellow Citizens: May this day which is set apart in recognition of one of the higher functions of the state recover and restore to us this former ideal. And accepting the inspiration and teaching of the present hour, may we understand better what is the abiding duty, and what the lasting honor of the sons of this ancient commonwealth.

MR. PRESIDENT: As suggested by Dr. Tucker, the Committee has been especially fortunate in being able to summon Mr. A. R. Spofford, librarian of the National library, to address you on this occasion.

Lord Bacon's classification of books was, "Some are to be tasted, others to be swallowed, and a few to be chewed and digested."

They credit Mr. Spofford with having "chewed and digested" the greater part of the books in the National library. He will tell you to-day, something of what he knows of the books he has devoured.

I have the honor of introducing to you Mr. Spofford, a native of New Hampshire, but a citizen of Washington.

Mr. Ainsworth R. Spofford, Librarian of Congress, delivered the concluding address on

THE WORLD OF BOOKS.

When I was honored by the invitation to take a part in this memorial service, I felt myself constrained to respond to the call by two considerations, mainly: first, as cherishing an active interest in libraries, in whose service the greater part of my life has been spent,—and, secondly, as contributing, in some slight degree, to a discharge of the debt which every man owes to the region of his nativity. As a son of New Hampshire, though removed in very early life from the state, I take pride in all that conduces to her

honor, her advancement, and her intelligence.   As a
librarian, it is most gratifying to me, in revisiting my
native State, to behold this fair temple of learning,
which you have carved out of New Hampshire granite,
and which you are now dedicating to the enlightenment of the legislative body, and of all who may in
the future use its stores.   It is equally gratifying to
recall the fact, that at the capital city of our republic,
another great library edifice now nears completion,
constructed of New Hampshire granite, from the
Concord quarries, as pure and white as the marble
walls of the capitol.

But, my friends, while we are justly solicitous to
provide these spacious and fire-proof repositories for
the books of the nation and of the state, and to adorn
their interiors with fitting ornaments and memorials,
we are not to forget the vast importance of filling
them with the best and most useful means of information.   To what purpose do we dedicate these
splendid temples to science and literature, unless we
are ready to provide liberally from the public funds,
to equip the government library with all the helps
which the legislator needs?   Indeed, when we reflect
that, in the last analysis, our laws are only the pro-
duct of our learning, (taking learning in its largest
sense,) we see that there is almost no knowledge
which can come amiss to those who make the laws.

It is trite enough for me to remind you of the
saying of that staunch Scotch republican, Andrew
Fletcher, who wrote, two centuries ago, that "if a
man were permitted to make all the ballads of a
nation, he need not care who should make the laws."

But the profounder meaning of the aphorism comes to us in the reflection that the sentiments of human sympathy, justice, virtue, and freedom, which inspire the best poetry of all nations, become sooner or later incarnated in their laws. If there are those narrow-minded enough to think that poetry is out of place in a legislative library, let them remember the debt the world owes to its great poets, from Homer down to Robert Burns. Even that simple little song—with the refrain—

> " Then let us pray that come it may,
>   As come it will, for a' that,
>   That man to man, the world o'er,
>   Shall brothers be, for a' that,"—

may have contributed almost as much to spread abroad the great doctrine of human equality, as the British Magna Charta, or the American Declaration of Independence. So, also, the German race are deeply indebted to the ballads of Schiller and Körner, and to the ideas of freedom which they have sown deep in the minds of men and women for two generations, for that measure of constitutional liberty which Germany now enjoys. And if we were to inquire whether books or battles have contributed the most to the progress of mankind, let us put into one scale the military achievements of all the con- querors, and into the other all the glorious literature of the world. If you doubt to which side the balance will incline, take the greatest of the warriors, him who won more battles than any man known to history, who marched from conquest to conquest, made him- self the master of France—then the autocrat of

Europe, and finally filled the world with his fame.
After sacrificing on the altar of his ambition, the
liberty of the press, the freedom of opinion, the ties
of marriage, the peace and welfare of his country,
and the lives of more than a million Frenchmen, he
went down at last, his many crimes against humanity
all unredeemed by that thin varnish which men call
glory—another witness to the truth, that justice still
rules the world.

All history and all literature conspire to teach
us that there is nothing at last but intellectual and
moral power, that is sacred or enduring among men.
We are the fortunate heirs of the intelligence of ages.
The thoughts and the facts that are garnered up in
books, are endowed with a life that is perennial.
Men may die, and legislators may perish, and libra-
rians are mortal : but libraries and literature are
immortal.   Even though the ever-gnawing tooth of
time should one day undermine this beautiful structure, and its granite walls should crumble to decay,—
yet through the ever-living power of the magic art
of printing, books will survive, and the thoughts of
the mind will far outlast towers of granite, and mon-
uments of marble.

"The art of writing," says a great scholar of our
century,—Thomas Carlyle, "certainly is the most
miraculous of all things which man has devised.   Of
all things which men can do or make here below, by
far the most momentous, wonderful, and worthy, are
the things we call books."   And indeed, when we
thoughtfully consider how wide and potential are the
uses of written speech, out of which the world of

books is made, it seems hardly possible to overstate the debt which we owe to authors. Books are the repositories of the wit and the wisdom of mankind. In their pages are stored the vast results of science, the long annals of history, the speculations of philosophers, the imaginations of poets, the discoveries of inventors, the narratives of travellers and voyagers, the lives of the illustrious, the laws and politics of nations, the observations of naturalists, the dreams of enthusiasts, the fascinating stories of fiction, the creations of graphic art, the harmonies of music, the homilies of theologians, the correspondence of men of letters, the verdicts of criticism, the traditions of the race, and the manifold languages of the world.

What to read, when to read, and how to read,— these are questions of vital importance to each one of us. While I have not the presumption to suppose that my ideas upon the choice of reading will present anything new, I must infer that the invitation to address you takes for granted on my part such fitness as a life spent among books and the readers of books may imply. All that any one can do for others is to suggest to them a clue, which, however feeble, has helped to guide his uncertain footsteps through that tangled maze of folly and wisdom which we call literature. And my excuse for venturing to address you upon a theme at once so exacting and so important, is that the suggestions which I may have to offer are the fruit of a candid observation, and an experience somewhat prolonged.

The art of reading to the best advantage implies the command of adequate time to read. The art of

having time to read lies in learning how to make the
most of our days.   Days are short, and time is fleet-
ing, but no one's day ever holds less than twenty-
four hours.   Engrossing as one's occupation may
be, it need never consume all the time remaining
from sleep, refreshment, and needful exercise.   The
trouble is, most persons think that the unappropria-
ted intervals when business waits are too brief and
fragmentary to be of any value to them.   They fear
that they will be interrupted before they have done
anything to the purpose, and so they do nothing.   No
one can make the most of life who has never learned
the supreme value of moments.   The half hour before breakfast, the fifteen minutes waiting for dinner, diligently given to the book one wishes to read,
will finish it in a few days, and make room for
another.   It is almost literally true, paradoxical as it
may seem, that the more you have to do, the more
you can do.   The idle person never knows how to
get ahead of his work ; the busy one always knows
how.   System and a strong purpose will work mira-
cles ; will go far toward achieving the impossible.
The busiest men I have known have frequently been
the best informed and the widest readers.

Let us suppose that you are determined to secure
two hours every day for self-culture ; that is equivalent to more than seven hundred hours a year—or to
three entire months of working time of eight hours
a day.   What could you not do in three months, if
you had all the time to yourself?   You could almost
learn a new language, or go far toward writing a
book, if need were ; and yet this two hours a day,

which would secure you three months of free time every year, is frittered away, you hardly know how, in aimless matters, that lead to nothing.

A famous writer, some of whose books we have all read, Bulwer-Lytton, devoted only four hours a day to writing; yet he produced more than sixty volumes of history, poetry, drama, and fiction, of singular literary merit. The great naturalist Darwin, a chronic sufferer from a depressing malady, counted two hours a good day's work; yet he produced results in the world of science which have made his name immortal. Be not over particular as to hours, or the time of day, but seize the unoccupied intervals and you will soon find that all hours are good for the muse. Have a purpose, and adhere to it with good-humored pertinacity. Be independent of the methods and opinions of others. The world of books, like the world of nature, was made for you; possess it in your own way. If you see no good in ancient history, or metaphysics, let them alone, and read books of art, or biography, or poetry, or travel. The world of letters is so related, that all roads cross and converge, like the paths that carry us over the surface of the globe on which we live. Many a reader has learned more of past ages from biographies than from any formal history, and it is a fact that many owe to the plays of Shakespeare nearly all the knowledge they possess of the history of England.

I look with some distrust upon many of the so-called "courses of reading." A great amount of time has been consumed in trying to compel the attention to reading through long and prosy didactic works written in a style the reverse of attractive, but believed to be packed full of learning. These courses, undertaken as a task, frequently break down before much progress has been made, thus ending in discouragement as well as disappointment; whereas, if a good book had been selected, written in a fresh and flowing style, and treating any topic whatever with adequate knowledge, it would have been eagerly read and assimilated. Time should be economized by selecting attractive intellectual pabulum—books which are known from the start to be full of good things—capable of nourishing the inner man, and, like a well-cooked and well-seasoned dish, both appetizing to the palate and comforting to the soul.

Suffer no man's prescription for a weak or deformed intellect to sway your choice, if you are conscious of your own mental strength and soundness. When you are weary or perplexed, who shall deny you the recreation of a chapter of Pickwick, or what Doctor Dry-as-dust shall compel you to read David Hume or Adam Smith, when you crave Tennyson or the Faust of Goethe?

It is unhappily true that books do not teach the use of books. It were easier, perhaps, in one sense, to tell what not to read, than to recommend what is best worth reading. In the publishing world, this is the age of compilation—not of creation. If we seek for great original works, if we must indeed go to the wholesale merchants to buy knowledge, since retail geniuses are worth but little, one must go back many years for his main selection of books. It would not be a bad rule, perhaps, for those who can read but little, to read no book until it has been published at least a year or two. This fever for the newest books is not a wholesome condition of the mind. And since a selection must indispensably be made, and that selection must, for the mass of readers, be so rigid and so small, why should valuable time be thrown away upon the untried and unproven writers of the day?

As the taste for reading is one of the greatest of human benefits, so the art of reading to the best advantage is one of the foremost things to be desired. One hears with dismay that the statistics of our popular libraries prove that about seventy-five per cent. of the books drawn from them are novels. While such aimless reading to be amused is doubtless better than no reading at all, it is nevertheless true that over-much reading of romances, especially at an early age, enervates the mind, weakens the will, makes dreamers instead of thinkers and workers, and fills the imagination with morbid and unreal views of life. Yet this habit of giving up all leisure hours to fiction is cultivated, more by the cheapness and notoriety of such works, and the absence of wise direction in other fields, than by any native tendency on the part of the young. People will always read the most that which is most put before them, if only the style be attractive.

A two-fold evil follows upon the reading of every unworthy book; in the first place, it absorbs the time which should be bestowed upon a worthy one; and secondly, it leaves the mind and heart unimproved, instead of conducing to the benefit of both. As there are few books more elevating than a really good novel, so there are none more fruitful of evil than a bad one.

Hazlitt says, "we owe everything to the authors of books, on this side barbarism." He who enters a great library walks among the silent ranks of the thinkers of all ages. However dull or vapid he may sometimes find the society of people, that of a well-selected library is never dull. In the world of books, your chosen companions will talk to you only when bidden, and whenever you hold converse with them, they always have something to say. The appreciative reader is never less alone than when alone. Surrounded by the spirits of the mighty dead, still surviving immortally in their works, while their mortal bodies are but dust, he drinks in the inspiration and the instruction that dwell among the leaves. His horizon insensibly widens as he reads, and from being a resident of Boston, or of Baltimore, or of Washington, he becomes a citizen of the world.

The reader who has held communion with many great writers will find his views correspondingly enlarged, and his mental vision cleared. The besetting conceit of opinion, the ignoble strife of warring sects and schools, are seen in their true light. He has read to little purpose who has not imbibed a charity as wide as the world, and an open-mindedness that is fatal to the slightest taint of bigotry. Much converse with books fills him with a sense of his own ignorance. The more he comes to know, the wider opens before him the illimitable realm of what is yet to be known. In the lowest deep which research the most profound can reach, there is a lower deep still unattained,—perhaps, even, unattainable.

But the fact that he cannot by any possibility master all human knowledge should not deter the student from making ever advancing inroads upon that domain. The vast extent of the world of books only emphasizes the need of making a wise selection from the mass. One of the commonest and most inconsiderate of the questions propounded to a librarian is this: "Do you ever expect to read all these books through"? And it is well answered by propounding another query—namely: "Did you ever read your dictionary through"? A great library is the scholar's dictionary—not to be read through, but to be able to put his finger on the fact or the thought he wants, just when it is wanted.

He must indispensably learn the art of skipping,—not only of skipping all the useless books (whose name is legion) but all the useless pages in which every book, almost, abounds. This art requires three things: Keen discernment, a practiced eye, and a resolute purpose to make the best use of time. As to the selection, while I am not of those who can see no merit save in books touched with the hoar frost of time, I have yet frequent cause to lament the prevalent rage for new books, when so many great masters lie unopened and unread. Schopenhauer tells us of the paramount importance of "acquiring the art *not* to read, or of not reading the books that occupy the public mind, make a noise in the world, and reach several editions in their first (and perhaps last) year of existence." Indeed there is of late, along with much good literature, a fearfully increasing number of books that are not useful. The spawn of cheap novels of second and third rate writers, the translations of Zola, Belot, Du Boisgobey, and others of the French erotic school, and their American imitators, some of whom surpass them in grossness, without any of their attractions of style, must be deplored by all who regard the moral and intellectual welfare of our people. Such publications degrade our literature, instead of ennobling and advancing it. Defend them as men may, with whatever glozing excuses, the books which belong to the lately prevalent bigamy school of fiction are not fit to be written, and not fit to be read. "The trail of the serpent is over them all." Let all friends of good literature, and all teachers and counsellors of the young, never cease to remember, that "the wisdom that is from above is first pure."

Another class of new literature is the sensational, which tends to vitiate the taste, as surely as the other does the morals. Why should one read such specimens of prose-run-mad as the novels of Augusta Evans, or Amélie Rives, such examples of morbid intellectual anatomy as the journal of Marie Bashkirtseff, or such pictures of over-wrought passion and vicious life as the stories of Edgar Saltus? These books, and others referred to, that tickle the palate for an hour, and perhaps leave a bad taste in the mouth, are good books to let alone. They have no staying qualities. Why waste the precious hours, which you will never see again, over things fit only to be forgotten, when the great masters of prose and verse are waiting to endow you with imperishable wit and wisdom?

Yet some readers will eagerly devour every novel of Miss Braddon, or "The Duchess," or the woman calling herself "Ouida," but they cannot appreciate the masterly fictions of Thackeray. I have known very good people who could not, for the life of them, find any humor in Dickens, but who actually enjoyed the forced wit of Mrs. Partington and Bill Nye. And you will find many a young lady of to-day who is content to remain ignorant of Homer and Shakespeare, but who is ravished by the charms of Trilby or the Heavenly Twins. But taste in literature, as in art, or in anything else, can be cultivated. Lay down the rule, and adhere to it, to read none but the best books, and you will before long lose all relish for the poor ones. Surely we all have cause to deprecate the remorseless flood of fictitious literature, in which better books are drowned.

Let no one be dismayed at the multitude of books, nor fear that with his small leisure, he will never be able to master any appreciable share of them. Few and far between are the great books of the world. The works which it is necessary to know may be comprised in a comparatively small compass. The rest are to be preserved in the great literary conservatories, some as records of the past, some as chronicles of the times, and not a few as models to be avoided. The Congressional Library at Washington (soon to have its own separate library building) is our great national conservatory of books. As the library of the government—that is of the whole people—it is properly inclusive of all the literature which the country produces, while all the other libraries are and must be more or less exclusive. No national library can ever be too large. In order that the completeness of the collection shall not fail, and to preserve the whole of our literature, it is put into the statute of copyright as a condition precedent of the exclusive right to multiply copies of any book. Apprehension is sometimes expressed that the library of the United States will become overloaded with trash, and so fail of its usefulness. 'Tis a lost fear. The public sense is continually winnowing and sifting the literature of every period, and to books and their authors, every day is the day of judgment.

Out of all the publications of any year, how many, think you, ever arrive at the honor of a republication at all? How many are thought worthy of a reprint by the readers of the generation immediately succeeding? And will any one learned in the history of literature tell us how many, out of the innumerable candidates for immortality, ever reach it, by the suffrage of each successive century, calling for continually new editions? Is not the fate of at least ninety-nine in the hundred writers, a swift passport to oblivion or (which is much the same thing) a place among the myriads of forgotten volumes which slumber on the shelves of the great libraries of the world?

It is the melancholy fate of most writers to survive their own literary reputation. Not the least among the evils of that "*furor scribendi*," that rage for writing which afflicts so large a portion of the human race, is the utter unconsciousness of its subjects as to the worthless or ephemeral character of their productions. A moderate acquaintance with the literature of the past would spare these unsophisticated authors the trouble of putting pen to paper. The discovery that what they are so eager to say has not only been said before, but a great deal better said than they can say it, might save them the mortification of publishing a neglected volume.

That learned French critic, Bishop Huet, was wont to say that all which has been written since the beginning of the world might easily be contained in nine or ten volumes in folio, *provided* nothing were said more than once. This little proviso is the key to that vast *copia librorum* under which we groan. So long as men go on repeating one another, so long will this redundancy of literature, which makes the despair of students, continue. All the ancient classics, both Greek and Latin, may be readily contained in a single glass case of very moderate dimensions; but. the million-fold echoes and re-echoes of the ancients which fill these twenty centuries—is there any library, however vast, which will hold the half of them?

Yet the world of books, vast and thickly peopled as it is, presents no anomaly, no exception to the laws which govern the genesis of nature and the growth of nations. Everywhere the chaff far exceeds the wheat. For a hundred blossoms, we gather but one ripe fruit. This ever-growing human race of ours goes swarming on, and how many, out of all the myriads that are born into the world, leave any mark

of greatness or of goodness to testify that they ever
lived at all? Shall the world of books be expected
to form the sole exception?

Shall we not rather use the brain that nature gave
us to make a wise choice of our intellectual companions? And here, let me say, no hard-and-fast
rule can be laid down, good for all readers. While
the world of books seems literally infinite, and we
are ever conscious that our opportunities are finite,
we may at least resolve to waste little time upon
writers who have not proven their claim to live in
literature. Find out how often any author's books
have been re-printed, in successive generations, and
you will have one standard of merit to which the
merely ephemeral writers cannot appeal. The sense
of the world is keen, and the survival of the fittest is
as certain as that art is long.

Next, there is no guide to that reading, which will
both interest and profit the reader, better than the
counsel embodied in these two lines of Shakespeare:

> "No profit grows where is no pleasure ta'en;
> In brief, sir, study what you most affect."

If this precept seems too free, it is to be borne in
mind that a book, in order to be relished and remem-
bered, must have some pleasing qualities to the
reader. Books that are read merely as task-work
profit little, in comparison with those which are
absorbed eagerly, and with a hungry mind. Now
the best books of the world are the histories, the
poems, and the stories which are the best told,—and
which will never want for readers, so long as the

generations of men shall endure. The taste for the
best literature will be formed fast enough, if only the
best be made as accessible as is the trash.

When Shakespeare would depict for us the sov-
ereign value of the intelligence which dwells in the
world of books, he says: "Ignorance is the curse of
God: Knowledge the wing wherewith we fly to
Heaven." And elsewhere, when he would describe
in few words a man deficient in understanding—he
says: "Sir, He hath never fed of the dainties which
are bred in a book." Gibbon declared—"A taste
for books is the pleasure and glory of my life :—I
would not exchange it for the wealth of the Indies."
And we remember the lofty panegyric of Words-
worth's sonnet:

"Blessings be with them, and eternal praise,
Who gave us nobler loves and nobler cares ;
The Poets, who on earth have made us heirs
Of truth and pure delight by heavenly lays."

In the companionship of books we move across
the centuries, and mingle with every race and every
age. They bring us acquainted with the fair forms
of truth and poetry, and reveal to us the genius and
the virtue that have illustrated the annals of mankind. Good books are among the few real things of
life : they are almost the only pleasure in which there
is no alloy. "Some books," says Petrarch, "teach
us how to live, and others how to die." Through
them, the spirits of the dead, not mortal, but immortal, hold free converse with us. Through them,
each one of us may become endowed with the storied
wisdom of six thousand years. The world of books

is a realm as large as the universe, and its noblest creations take hold on the infinite. They open to us inexhaustible treasures of learning: they awaken the reason, they kindle the imagination, they cultivate the memory, they refine the taste, they delight us in health, they comfort us in sickness, they enliven the fancy, they quicken the conscience, they purify the soul; they cheer the desponding, they strengthen the weak, they lighten our cares, they soften our griefs, they enhance our joys—they energize and ennoble the mind. They, and they alone, hold that which is imperishable in man; that which survives centuries, conquers oblivion, and triumphs over the grave.

APPENDIX.

JOINT RESOLUTION authorizing the governor and council to procure plans and estimates for additions to the state house.

Resolved by the Senate and House of Representatives in General Court convened:

That the governor and council are hereby authorized to expend a sum of money not exceeding five hundred dollars, to be used in procuring plans and estimates for additional facilities in the state house for library and other purposes, and also plans and estimates for a separate building to be used for the same purposes, and submit their report to the next legislature.

That the governor is hereby authorized to draw his warrant for the same out of any money in the treasury not otherwise appropriated.

Approved August 16, 1889.

AN ACT for the erection of a state library building.

Be it enacted by the Senate and House of Representatives in General Court convened:

SECTION 1. That the sum of one hundred and seventy-five thousand dollars be and hereby is raised and appropriated for the purchase of two tracts of land situate on the corner of State and Park streets in Concord, and the erection of a building thereon, in accordance with the plan of A. P. Cutting, of Worcester, Mass., referred to in and annexed to the report of the commission appointed to procure plans and estimates for additional facilities for the public library, and other purposes.

SECT. 2. The state treasurer is hereby authorized, under the direction of the governor and council to borrow said sum of one hundred and seventy-five thousand dollars on the credit of the state; and to issue bonds or certificates of indebtedness therefor, in the name and on the behalf of the state, payable in twenty years from the first day of July, 1891, at a rate of interest not exceeding four per cent. per annum, payable semi-annually on the first days of January and July of each year; such bonds to have interest warrants or coupons attached thereto; said coupons to be signed by the state treasurer; said bonds and coupons to be made payable at such place as the governor and council shall designate.

SECT. 3. Said bonds shall be designated, "State Library Bonds," and shall be signed by the treasurer and countersigned by the governor, and shall be deemed a pledge of the faith and credit of the state. The secretary of state shall keep a record of all the bonds countersigned by the governor, showing the number and amount of each bond, the time of countersigning, the time when payable, and the date of the delivery to the state treasurer. The treasurer shall keep a record of all bonds disposed of by him, showing the number thereof, the name of the person to whom sold, the amount received for the same, the date of the sale and the time when payable. The treasurer may negotiate and sell such bonds to the best advantage for the state, but no bond shall be sold for less than its par value, nor shall such bonds be loaned, pledged, or hypothecated in any way whatever.

Sect. 4. That His Excellency the Governor, with the advice and consent of the council, be authorized to appoint four commissioners, only two of whom shall belong to the same political party, whose duty it shall be to make all contracts necessary for the erection, building, and completion of said state library building upon the plot of ground named in section 1 of this act, and in accordance with said plan to procure all necessary specifications for the full completion of said building under said plan. No contract by them made shall be of any binding force until first submitted to and approved by the governor and council, nor shall such contract be made until they have advertised for at least thirty days in not less than three papers in this state for sealed proposals under said plan and specifications for the entire construction of said building in one contract, or in several contracts for the different classes of work to be done, and such contract or contracts shall be made with the lowest responsible bidders complying with the terms of this act in relation to the amount of bonds required to guarantee the completion of said contract ; and it shall be the further duty of said commissioners to superintend the erection, building, and completion of said library building, and they shall receive for their services each the sum of three dollars per day when employed and their expenses, and their bills shall be approved by the governor and council ; and the governor shall draw his orders upon the state treasurer for the amounts due from time to time upon said bills, and the treasurer shall pay the same out of any money provided for in this act. Said commissioners, or either of them, may be removed at any time by the governor and council.

Sect. 5. Said commissioners shall have power and authority to purchase for and on behalf of the state the land recommended by the commission and named in section 1 of this act, subject to the approval of the governor and council.

Sect. 6. In case said commissioners shall be unable to purchase such land for the state at a price which they deem reasonable, they are hereby fully authorized and empowered to take and appropriate the same for the use of the state, for the purpose aforesaid ; and if such land is so taken and appropriated for the use of the state, said commissioners shall apply to the county commissioners for the county of Merrimack to assess the damages to the owner or owners of such land, and said county commissioners, upon reasonable notice to all persons interested and a hearing thereon, shall assess and award damages to the owner or owners of such land, for so much land as the commissioners hereby appointed shall designate as necessary and convenient for the purposes aforesaid. Said assessment and award of the county commissioners shall be in writing, and filed in the office of the city clerk of said Concord within ten days after the same is completed, which shall contain a particular description by metes and bounds of the land so taken, as well as of the damages and the persons to whom the same is awarded. And upon payment or tender to the owner or owners of the land of the sums so assessed, the title to the land so taken shall be vested in the state.

Sect. 7. Such land-owner, or other party interested, shall have the right to appeal from said assessment and award to the supreme court in said county of Merrimack, and to an assessment of said damages by a jury on such appeal, by filing in the office of the clerk of said court a petition in proper form for that purpose, within sixty days after the filing of said assessment and award of said county commissioners in the office of the city clerk as aforesaid.

Sect. 8. The governor shall draw his orders on the state treasurer for the amounts that may be or become due from time to time, under the contracts of the commissioners hereby appointed, for the purposes aforesaid, after said bills shall have been duly approved by the governor and council, to an amount not exceeding one hundred and seventy-five thousand dollars.

Approved March 12, 1891.

AN ACT in addition and supplemental to chapter 13 of the Laws of 1891, entitled "An act for the erection of a state library building."

Be it enacted by the Senate and House of Representatives in General Court convened.

SECTION 1. That the sum of seventy-five thousand dollars be and the same is hereby appropriated for the purpose of completing and furnishing the state library building and the grounds about the same, to be expended under the direction of the commission appointed in pursuance of section 4 of chapter 13, Laws of 1891, entitled an "An act for the Erection of a State Library Building," and in accordance with said act.

SECT. 2. The state treasurer is hereby authorized, under the direction of the governor and council, to borrow the sum of seventy-five thousand dollars on the credit of the state; and to issue bonds or certificates of indebtedness therefor, in the name and on the behalf of the state, payable in twenty years from the first day of July, 1893, at a rate of interest not exceeding four per cent. per annum, payable semi-annually on the first days of January and July of each year; such bonds to have interest warrants or coupons attached thereto; said coupons to be signed by the state treasurer; said bonds and coupons to be made payable at such place as the governor and council shall designate.

SECT. 3. Said bonds shall be designated "State Library Bonds," and shall be signed by the treasurer and countersigned by the governor, and shall be deemed a pledge of the faith and credit of the state. The secretary of state shall keep a record of all the bonds countersigned by the governor, showing the number and amount of each bond, the time of countersigning, the time when payable, and the date of the delivery to the state treasurer. The treasurer shall keep a record of all bonds disposed of by him, showing the number thereof, the name of the person to whom sold, the amount received for the same, the date of the sale, and the time when payable. The treasurer may negotiate and sell such bonds to the best advantage for the state, but no bond shall be sold for less than its par value, nor shall such bonds be loaned, pledged, or hypothecated in any way whatever.

SECT. 4. All premiums realized from the sale of the state library bonds, issued under and by virtue of chapter 13, Laws of 1891, and under this act, are hereby appropriated for the uses set forth in section 1 of this act, and to be expended by said commissioners agreeably to this act, and said act of 1891.

SECT. 5. The governor shall draw his orders on the state treasurer for the amounts that may be or become due from time to time, under the contracts of said commissioners, for the purposes aforesaid, after said bills shall have been duly approved by the governor and council, to an amount not exceeding the several sums appropriated by this act, and said chapter 13, Laws of 1891.

SECT. 6. This act is in addition and supplemental to chapter 13, Laws of 1891.

Approved February 14, 1893.

———

AN ACT in amendment of chapter 8 of the Public Statutes, and chapter 31 of the Laws of 1893, relating to the state library.

Be it enacted by the Senate and House of Representatives in General Court convened.

SECTION 1. Section 8 of chapter 8 of the Public Statutes is hereby amended so as to read as follows: "Sect. 8. They may dispose, by sale or exchange, of all or any part of the surplus state publications, which have been from time to time deposited in the state library in accordance with the laws of the state, and of such other books, pamphlets, charts, documents, or duplicates thereof, as they deem unnecessary for the uses of the library."

SECT. 2. Section 16 of chapter 8 of the Public Statutes is hereby amended to read as follows : "Sect. 16. The governor, councillors, members, and clerks of the legislature, during sessions, state officials, the judges of the supreme court, and such other persons as the trustees shall designate, may take books, maps, charts, and other documents from the library, subject to such rules and regulations as the trustees shall prescribe."

SECT. 3. Section 18 of chapter 8 of the Public Statutes is hereby amended by inserting after the word "studies," in the last line thereof, the words "and all other printed matter of the institution." So that said section shall read as follows : "Sect. 18. The principal of each college, academy, seminary, or other institution of learning, incorporated by the laws of this state, shall annually and before the first day of November of each year, forward to the state librarian for the state library two copies, and to the New Hampshire Historical Society two copies, of each printed catalogue of its officers and students and courses of study, and all other printed matter of the institution published during the year ending on that date."

SECT. 4. Section 6 of chapter 31 of the Laws of 1893 is hereby amended so as to read as follows : "Sect. 6. The public printer shall give the state librarian seasonable notice of every state or department publication that is delivered to him to be printed, and of the time that same will go to press. Upon receipt of such notice the state librarian shall notify the secretary of state of the number of additional copies of every such publication that will be required for sale or exchange for the benefit of the state library, and thereupon the secretary of state shall cause such number of copies to be printed, bound, and delivered to the state librarian, in addition to the number of copies otherwise required to be printed by law; *provided*, however, that such requisition shall be made while the work may be done without extra expense on account of composition, and *provided* that the several state departments shall not receive a less number of copies for the official distribution than is now authorized by law."

SECT. 5. The residue of all state or department publications remaining in the hands of the secretary of state after distribution by him as required by law, shall be forthwith deposited in the state library, to be disposed of as required by law.

SECT. 6. Foreign corporations doing business in this state shall file with the state librarian on or before the first day of January in each year, all printed reports of their condition issued by them during the twelve months preceding.

SECT. 7. This act shall take effect upon its passage.

Approved February 13, 1895.